ETHIC$ +®

IN BIG BOX RETAIL

Your Compass for Making Ethical Decisions

By

Kevin McNabb

ETHIC$ + ® In Big Box Retail – Your Compass for Making Ethical Decisions

Copyright © 2023 Kevin D. McNabb, Etobicoke, Ontario, Canada M8Y 2Z5

Published by Kevin McNabb International Press

Toronto, Ontario M8Y2Z5

All rights reserved. No portion of this publication may be reproduced, stored in a retrieval system, or transmitted in any form by any means – electronic, mechanical, photocopying, recording, or another – except in brief quotations in printed reviews, without the prior written permission of the publisher.

Project Editor – Maya "Pooh Bear" McNabb

Book jacket designed by Sherri Marteney at Fiverr.com

ISBN: 9798373429078

Dedication

This book is dedicated to Brad Hanson, mentor, coach, and special friend. Please rest in peace, you will truly be missed.

Acknowledgments

I would like to say a special thank you to:

Pearce Jarvis, who helped me experience different roles of retail at a store level.

Tim Ravenhill & Dan Harrington, who took a chance by hiring me in a retail management role.

Marvin Ellison for his global direction and leadership.

and Maya Nicole McNabb, my daughter, thanks for making me laugh.

Table of Contents

Dedication 2

Acknowledgments 3

Help, I Cannot Find Ethics in Retail? 5

    The Retail Sector is Not Exempt from this "List of Shame" 7

    Do We Have an Ethical Dilemma Within the Retail Sector? 8

    Dr. Joseph Fletcher – The Founder of the Situational Ethics Movement 11

    What Would Happen If a Retail Associate Always Did What Was Most Convenient? 14

    What Would Happen If a Retail Associate Believed That They Have to Do Whatever Is Necessary to Seek Victory? 14

    What's That? Is the Global Retail Sector Altering Its Behavior? 15

    Why the Global Retail Sector Should Not Follow the Trend of the Global Marketplace 17

    We Should Take This Personally as Retail Associates 20

    Ethics and the Final Word 20

    Observations from the Retail Floor 22

- How About an Ethical "Gold Standard" for Retail? 25
  - The Key Reasons Why Ethics Should Make a Difference to a Retail Associate 27
  - Powerful Reasons Why You and I as Retail Associates Should Embrace this Gold Standard..32
    - This Ethical Compass is Accepted by the Majority of Retail Associates....................32
    - The Ethical Compass is Straightforward as well as Simple to Comprehend 35
  - With This Ethical Compass Everyone Wins ..36
  - This Ethical Compass Will Always Point You in The Right Direction 39
  - The "Gold Standard" for Best Places to Work For 39
    - 2021 Top 100 Retailers 46
    - 2021 World's Most Ethical Companies 46
  - Observation from a Retail Associate............48
    - The 30 Worst Things About Working in Retail 49
- Why the Ethical "Gold Standard" Begins with You 53
  - Human Experience – The Four Classes 56

The Six Human Needs 59

The Reason Why Most People Love or Hate to Try and Do Things.. 67

Adopting the Ethical "Gold Standard" 74

As a Retail Associate, I Truly Would Like to be Valued 74

As a Retail Associate, I Truly Wish to be Appreciated... 76

As a Retail Associate I Truly Wish to be Trusted 78

As a Retail Associate, I Truly Wish to be Respected.. 79

   10 Rules for Respect.................................. 80

As a Retail Associate, I Wish to be Understood 82

As a Retail Associate, I Truly Do Not Want Others to Take Advantage of Me 83

Understanding the Value of People 85

7 Reasons Why a People-First Culture is Changing How Leaders Manage Employees 87

   Observations from a Retail Associate 88

How to Live the Ethical "Gold Standard" at the Highest Level 89

   The Golden Rule and the Life of J.C. Penney 98

- Observations from a Retail Associate 102

What to Watch Out for When Adopting the Ethical "Gold Standard" 103

- Condition #1 – Pressure 104
- Condition #2 – Pleasure 110
- Condition #3 – Power................................113
- Condition #4 – Pride..................................115
- Condition #5 – Priorities............................117
- Observations from a Retail Associate 119

Carpe Diem and the Ethical "Gold Standard" 120

- Observations from a Retail Associate 137

The Following Steps Will Help You Implement the Ethical "Gold Standard" 139

- Observations from a Retail Associate 159

Conclusion: Pursue the Ethical Gold Standard Life..161

Marvin Ellison – Example of a Leader that Lives a Gold Standard 3.0 Life..................................167

About the Author 169

End Notes..171

Help, I Cannot Find Ethics in Retail?

How would you describe the condition of ethics in the retail world today? If you happen to be like many people, you are ashamed and therefore are sick and tired of men and women telling lies and being unethical.

Lying and unethical practices have spread throughout every facet of our lives. Let us look.

Traditional businesses: Equifax, Fox Entertainment Group, NFL, University of Phoenix, Electronic Arts (EA), Foxconn Technology Group, Sprint, Vice Media, Spirit Airlines, Cigna, Wells Fargo, The Trump Organization, Sears Holdings, Uber, Comcast, Monsanto, CenturyLink, Facebook, United Airlines and The Weinstein Company. [i]

In the past these names would have been Enron, Arthur Anderson, WorldCom, Adelphia Communications, Wal-Mart, Trafigura, DynCorp, Chevron, Blackwater, Dow Chemical, Union Carbide, Siemens, IBM, Halliburton, Raytheon, to list but a few examples.

These ethical problems we are witnessing are not restricted to just the business world.

Education Systems – Ethical Issues in Education – Barriers to Learning in Schools (choice of instructor /or teacher, issues of discipline, Ethnic and Social Diversity, Grading, etc.)

Religions – Just look at the recent allegations of child molestation, embezzlement, or worse in the Catholic Church.

Politicians – Let us make this easy by saying key leaders in the Republican and Democratic parties.

Financial System - Irresponsible financiers, Misleading borrowers of funds, Misinformation concerning loans, Illegal financing, Discriminatory financial conditions, Abuse of financial trust, Incompetent financial advisers, Professional misconduct of financial agents, Temptations of financial occupations.

It is fair to say that one reason the global stock markets have so much day-to-day fluctuation is a direct result of lack of trust.

Criminal Justice System – How about misconduct and corruption in law enforcement, lawyers, and judges.

Sports – Lance Armstrong, OJ Simpson, Pete Rose, Tiger Woods, Barry Bonds, Tonya Harding and Nancy Kerrigan, PENN State, 1918 Chicago Black Sox to name a few.

The Retail Sector is Not Exempt from this *"List of Shame"*

Sadly, each day, somewhere around the world, unethical business practice happens within the Retail Sector.

Sure, several retailers have been accused of unethical behavior such as: Abercrombie and Fitch, Walmart, Forever 21, T.J. Maxx, Ross Stores, Macy's, Zara, Mango, Topshop, Uniqlo. [ii]

How about Amazon, ASDA Walmart, Nestle, Tesco and Coca-Cola. [iii]

It should not come as a surprise to you to find out that most of these retailers have had their ethics questioned. However, bear in mind one key element, a retail company is merely an entity comprised of a bunch of human beings. A therein lies the problem.

"The best thing about being part of a retailer is the people. The worst part about being part of a retailer is the people.
□ *"*- Kevin McNabb

Do We Have an Ethical Dilemma Within the Retail Sector?

Numerous discussions about ethics and unethical practices are established based on arguments about the suitable definition. Ethics is unique among professions in that experts frequently are unable to agree on a standard definition of an ethical dilemma. Therefore, for the purpose of this book, I am going to utilize the following definition of "*ethical dilemma.*"

"This is an ethical problem in which the ethical choice involves ignoring a powerful non-ethical consideration. Do the right thing, but lose your job, a friend, a lover, or an opportunity for advancement. A non-ethical consideration can be powerful and important enough to justify choosing it over the strict ethical action."[iv]

Exactly why has ethics over the last few decades in the Retail Sector been in such bad condition?

Let us look at several reasons why a Retail Associate would make unethical choices.

When a Retail Associate makes unethical choices, he/she does so for one of three reasons:

1. **Regrettably, the Average Retail Associate Truly Does What's Most Hassle-free**
    a. As a Retail Associate, we continuously fail individual ethics tests.
    b. As a Retail Associate, we will do things even though we understand that they are inappropriate.
    c. As a Retail Associate, we will do these inappropriate things,

perhaps because we believe that we will not get caught.
   d. As a Retail Associate, we use the justification of being stressed to cut corners and we justify that it is going to happen just one more time. Is this the ethical way of dealing with stress?
2. **Retail Associates Will Do Whatever They Believe They Must Do to Obtain a Victory**
   a. Most Retail Associates detest losing.
   b. Most successful Retail Associates that I know desire to win through personal and organizational achievement. However, the downside is that many believe they need to choose between being ethical and being successful.
   c. Many Retail Associates believe that embracing ethics would limit their choices, their opportunities, and their ability to succeed in the Retail Sector. It is the old suspicion that good guys finish last.
   d. If a Retail Associate believes that they have just two choices, to win by doing whatever it takes, even

if it is unethical or to have ethics and lose, they are faced with a moral dilemma. Few Retail Associates set out with the desire to be dishonest, but no one wants to lose.

3. **A Retail Associate Will Certainly Justify Their Options with Relativism**
    a. Many Retail Associates decide to cope with such no-win scenarios simply by choosing what is appropriate in the moment, based on their circumstances. Their own perception that principles such as right and wrong, goodness and badness, or truth and falsehood are not absolute, however, varies from culture to culture and situation to situation.

Dr. Joseph Fletcher – The Founder of the Situational Ethics Movement

Joseph Fletcher, an Anglican theologian, developed situation ethics in the 1960's after critiquing legalism and antinomianism. Legalism is the belief that there are fixed moral laws that must always be obeyed.

Antinomianism is the belief that there are no fixed moral principles, and that ethics should be spontaneous.

Fletcher believed that neither legalism nor antinomianism provided a sound basis for ethics and advocated *"situationism"* as a compromise. His book, **Situation Ethics**, was the centerpiece of his critique and founded much of the modern situation ethics movement.

According to Fletcher, decision-making should be based on the circumstances of a situation, and not on fixed law. He believed that truth is relative, and that love is the only absolute. Thus, he believed that if love is the intention, the end justifies the means.

Ironically, Fletcher claims he founded his model on a biblical statement found in 1 John 4:8: *"God is love."* Yet he did not realize that the same book says commandment keeping shows our love for God (1 John 5:3) and that God never approves a law breaking. Indeed, such conduct is sinful (1 John 3:4). [v]

What eventually happened to Fletcher? His conclusion that God's Word was not enough to guide decision-making led him to become an avid supporter of euthanasia and abortion. He died in 1991 an atheist.

The Retail Sector unfortunately has not been spared the spread of "*situational ethics.*"

The outcome is ethical turmoil. Each Retail Associate has his/her own ethical standards, which usually transform from situation to situation.

It is fascinating to note that even though our decisions at one time were based on ethics, now ethics are based on our decisions. If it is good for me, then it is good. Where is this trend likely to end?

Let us look at what would happen if we applied this trend to the Retail Sector:

What Would Happen If a Retail Associate Always Did What Was Most Convenient?

What if all of us decided, as Retail Associates, to just manage each situation based on what was most convenient to us? Not over a brief period, but over an extended period. What do you think would happen to our relationships with our fellow employees? What about our relationship with our management team? How about our relationship with our customers? Answer: **Total disaster.**

What Would Happen If a Retail Associate Believed That They Have to Do Whatever Is Necessary to Seek Victory?

As a Retail Associate, our entire business relies on the relationships we have with other employees, management, and customers. As Retail Associates, if we tried to "*win*" each transaction or interaction with our customers, over time those relationships would die off. The best way to make sure that both your business and your relationships with other employees or customers is to seek out a win-win scenario for each transaction and/or interaction.

What If a Retail Associate Decided to Handle a No-Win Situation by Deciding What Was Right in The Moment, Or According to Their Circumstances?

As a Retail Associate, or even as a human being for that matter, waiting until the last moment to decide how to handle a situation without a proper moral compass will end in disaster sooner rather than later.

There needs to be a better way. Good News: There is.

What's That? Is the Global Retail Sector Altering Its Behavior?

I am aware that sometimes it may not appear this way; however, there seems to be an ever-increasing desire for unethical practices in business, and this reaches the summit of the Retail Sector.

With regards to retail, the entire world is shrinking; the international retail marketplace is increasingly more accessible with each day and every transaction. Even though retail business has brought people closer together, culture and traditions will always be in some sort of conflict.

Whenever you are working in retail business with people of other cultures, it is especially important to understand the differences. It is vital that you recognize that the international retail marketplace is a diverse marketplace, and that your potential customers may possess different perspectives on ethics and appropriate behavior than those with which you are familiar.

As Retail Associates, we are part of multi-million-dollar opportunities (some cases billion-dollar) and thus our actions should reflect the highest ethical standards expected on the global stage.

It is exciting to realize there is a desire to change ethics in our culture. The sad news is that most

Retail Associates do not seem to understand how to make that transition.

Keep in mind that the moment you step into the global Retail Sector, you really need to be in a global frame of mind. Bid farewell to conventional North American jargon and opt for common, direct, and courteous ways of communicating your thoughts, beliefs, and ideas.

Furthermore, take the time to research the country and the culture of those with whom you will be interacting. It is important that you know the boundaries when it comes to asking personal questions. What you think is polite chitchat could be an offensive question to someone else.

Getting into the global Retail Sector is a challenging, but extremely rewarding, endeavor if you do it right. Just be sure that you are informed and ready to take on the responsibilities involved, and you will find the global Retail Sector is a wonderful place for your business to be.

Why the Global Retail Sector Should Not Follow the Trend of the Global Marketplace

So why shouldn't the Retail Sector follow the trend of the global marketplace where it pertains to ethics?

Look at how the global marketplace is currently trying to address the problem of ethics in business. They are:

- Asking other individuals that are not part of their organization to take on the responsibility of instructing their organization about ethics.
- Some companies have outsourced the task of training ethics to their employees, so that in the event of wrongdoing, the company can attempt to evade punishment for failure to comply with governmental guidelines.
- Ignore the problem, or insufficiently reprimanding the individual for unacceptable behavior.

Instead of the company taking a proactive approach to teach their employees proper ethical standards, some global companies have decided to deal with ethical offenders only when caught.

This seems a lot like closing the barn doors after the horses have escaped.

Depending on the laws of the municipality, state, or country to address the problem.

Here is the saddest of them all. Some companies have given up entirely on deciding what is ethical and instead are using what is legal as their standard for decision-making. Any wonder why we have the problem we have in the global marketplace?

Let us apply these "*solutions*" to the Retail Sector. How do you think these solutions would be received within our global community?

Would you really want to hand over to an "*unknown*" source how your business should be run and how your customers and employees are treated? I hope that your answer is no. If you are unsure of this answer, you may want to think about a career change outside the Retail Sector.

How about waiting until someone gets caught, even though you know that you are doing something wrong. Is that the way you would want your business to be run, or have your employees run your business?

Once again, I hope your answer is "*No.*"

Would you like to rely on the law to manage your business? Since most retail companies represent National, if not, international businesses, relying on the law of different states or nations becomes next to impossible, if not reprehensible.

What do I mean by that? The last place a retail company wants to leave their destiny is in the hands of any government.

We Should Take This Personally as Retail Associates

In today's modern society, we believe ethics is either a business or political issue. It is neither, it is a personal issue.

As Retail Associates we say we would like integrity. However, at the same time, ironically, a large number of Retail Associates do not always act with the kind of integrity they expect from others.

As an example, the Retail Associate who cheats on his taxes or steals office supplies from the store demands honesty and integrity from the corporation whose stock he buys, the politician he votes for, and the customer he deals with at the store level.

It is an easy task to talk about ethics and even easier to be embarrassed as a Retail Associate who falls short in an ethics evaluation, particularly when we have been violated by the wrongdoing of other Retail Associates. It is more difficult to make ethical choices in our own lives. When we as Retail Associates are faced with objectionable alternatives, what are we going to do?

Ethics and the Final Word

I recognize the need to constantly strive to be ethical, and it is my personal belief that you do as well. I am also a firm believer that it must be possible to do what is right 100% of the time and still be a successful and profitable Retail business.

Paradigm: Retail Associates who are committed to carrying out what is right and have a personal dedication to social responsibility, and who consistently act on it, will help their Retail store be more profitable overall than those who do not.

Now I am not implying that if you embrace ethical behavior, you will automatically have a successful and profitable Retail business. That would be foolish. However, it will create a solid foundation on which to build a successful and profitable Retail business.

Let us discuss returning to fundamentals. Just how can you become aware of what is right? Precisely how do you find the way through the most challenging of stressed-filled situations?

Exactly where can you locate a standard that will work in every situation, a guide that will assist you to sleep nicely at night, succeed as a Retail Associate, transform your relationships, and have confidence that you are doing all you can every time?

Answer: **Read on**.

Observations from the Retail Floor

All of us as Retail Associates always possess a great ethical obligation to try and do what is right. One element, however, is standing in our way: we are human beings!

Regrettably, for as long as there are men and women involved with Retail business, we are going to continue to have questionable ethics in the Retail Sector. That is, unless "*we*" as individual men and women, as well as the Retail Sector, decide to change.

Most Retail Associates desire to change their work environment, local community, or family situation without having to change themselves. *News Flash:* **It does not work that way.**

We must stop spending time attempting to change others and begin focusing all our time on changing ourselves. If enough Retail Associates did that, the impact would be exponential.

Are there ethically questionable Retail Companies? Probably. However, the challenge is that some Retail Companies have some ethically questionable employees associated with their organization.

How can we change as individuals and ensure that "*we*" are not part of the problem, but part of the solution?

To start, under no circumstances do anything because it is convenient, where it pertains to running your Retail business. Always do what is "*right*," even if it impacts your Retail business financially. Do not think short-term; always have a big picture attitude.

Look for a win-win scenario in all your interactions. Make sure that with this strategy, the other person wins first. This will go a long way towards building stronger relationships with fellow employees and customers.

Make decisions ahead of time on how you will handle situations within your Retail business and communicate them to all employees. This way, you will not be forced to continually make decisions on the fly that will lead to unethical behavior.

Do not worry about what other Retailers are doing in the marketplace. Only worry about what you are doing. Clean up your own backyard, before even thinking about pointing to someone else's.

Be fully responsible for your Retail business. Do not rely on others to determine what is right and wrong. If you see something wrong in your Retail business (this includes fellow employees and management), make the correction and move on. Waiting until it corrects itself is a recipe for disaster.

There is a solution to every problem. You just must take a moment and look for it. Be part of the solution, not the problem.

How About an Ethical "Gold Standard" for Retail?

How would you as a Retail Associate rate yourself regarding integrity and ethics? In the Retail Sector, many statistics are measured, such as revenue, margin, how well we focus on the customer, and in some cases personal and professional development. Rarely does one measure their level of integrity and ethics. But what if you did? What if you knew where you stood today from an ethical perspective, as well as where you would like to be? Would this be beneficial to you and your organization? Of course, it would let us look at ourselves for a moment.

It all starts at home. Far too often we are concerned about what others think of us, or how they would react to what we are thinking. This being the case, I highly recommend that we all start by cleaning up our own ethical backyard first. Then we do not have to worry about what others think about us, because we will know that we are on a strong ethical path.

For this discussion, allow us to sort Retail Associates into one of the five diverse categories below:

1. As a Retail Associate, I am always ethical.
2. As a Retail Associate, I am primarily ethical.

3. As a Retail Associate, I am ethical to some degree.
4. As a Retail Associate, I am frequently ethical.
5. As a Retail Associate, I am never ever ethical.

So, which one of the statements above is applicable to you? Precisely how would you define yourself? How would others define you? Now I am not asking what statement you would like to best describe you, however, that would be important to know from a growth perspective. Be honest with yourself and place a checkmark next to the statement that is most applicable to you. (It is OK, no one is looking!)

The Key Reasons Why Ethics Should Make a Difference to a Retail Associate

Now, hopefully you have been honest with yourself and placed a checkmark next to one of the statements above that best describes you. Let us now look at how men and women in the Retail Sector view ethics.

The vast majority of Retail Associates will always place themselves within the first or second category (ethical or primarily ethical). Most men and women attempt to be ethical much of the time.

All Retail Associates who consider themselves to be *"primarily ethical,"* do so because of individual opportunism. Discord is undesirable. Exercising self-discipline is undesirable. Being defeated is unfavorable. A wide variety of Retail Associates who consider themselves to be *"primarily ethical,"* choose this direction simply because they do not wish to cope with those distractions.

All Retail Associates feel that staying *"primarily ethical"* is okay, except in cases where these men and women happen to be on the losing end of another individual's breach in ethics.

One guideline can assist Retail Associates to make the move from *"primarily ethical"* to *"at all times ethical"* and eliminate the gap between the first two categories.

Imagine if you happen to be presented with a code of conduct or a moral compass to help you govern all your ethical decision-making, would you use it?

What if this moral compass was accessible to the masses and transcended all global cultures? Now would you use it?

Do you believe a global moral compass really exists? One does: It exists perfectly in what we have coined the *"Golden Rule."*

Idiom: *"do unto others as you would have them do unto you"*

What would the Retail Sector be like if all Retail Associates behaved toward others as they would like to have others behave towards them?

The Golden Rule is mentioned throughout every ancient writing about behavioral precepts (including the New Testament, Talmud, Koran, and the Analects of Confucius). Among the earliest appearances in English is Earl Rivers' translation of a saying of Socrates (Dictes and Sayenges of the Philosophirs, 1477): "*Do to other as thou wouldst they should do to thee and do to none other but as thou wouldst be done to.*" It is so well known that it is often shortened.

By inquiring, "*How would I like to be treated in this situation?*" You have accessed one of the most powerful principles in the world.

As a Retail Associate, are you considering disregarding my pronouncement? If this is the situation, then you could be ensnared in the entanglement of modern day thinking on ethics.

Permit me to demonstrate why the "*Golden Rule*" can be used as an ethical compass and why it will always point you in the right direction.

Individual Rules? How About One Guideline for Everyone?

An example of the Golden Rule is available in each culture. In the chart below you will see several adaptations to the Golden Rule:

See below for Global Religions and descriptions.

Bahai - *"And if thine eyes be turned towards justice, choose thou for thy neighbor that which thou choosest for thyself."* [vi]

Buddhism - *"Hurt not others with that which pains yourself."* [vii]

Christianity - *"Whatever you want men to do to you, do also to them."* [viii]

Confucianism - *"What you do not want done to yourself, do not do to others."* [ix]

Commonsensism - *"Treat people the way you'd like to be treated."* [x]

Hinduism - *"This is the sum of duty; do naught unto others what you would not have them do unto you."* [xi]

Islam - *"No one of you is a believer until he loves for his neighbor what he loves for himself."* [xii]

Jainism - *"A man should wander about treating all creatures as he himself would be treated."* [xiii]

Judaism - *"What is hateful to you, do not do to your fellow man. This is the entire law; all the rest is commentary."* [xiv]

Yoruba Proverb (Nigeria) - *"One going to take a pointed stick to pinch a baby bird should first try it on himself to feel how it hurts."* [xv]

Zoroastrianism - *"Whatever is disagreeable to yourself, do not do unto others."* [xvi]

Based upon the examples above, it is clear to me that the Golden Rule is available to virtually every culture and religion, as well as available to all Retail Associates no matter where they reside on the planet. Without question, the Golden Rule is the best example of a worldwide guideline for ethics that is possible to find. There are only two significant factors when it comes to the subject of ethics:

1. A standard to follow.
2. The will to follow it.

Ethics is related to how we as Retail Associates satisfy the challenging task of carrying out the appropriate thing when that *"thing"* will impact us much more as compared to what we are prepared to pay.

Truth is there are two elements to ethics: the first consists of the capability to be able to determine correct from incorrect, acceptable from unacceptable, and congruity from incongruity. The second entails the dedication to carry out what is appropriate, good as well as correct. Ethics requires us as Retail Associates to act; it is not just a subject to consider or dispute.

Powerful Reasons Why You and I as Retail Associates Should Embrace this Gold Standard

Some of you may be thinking, *"Kevin, how can you be so naïve?"* I recognize that not every person is searching for a straightforward, sensible, and relevant guideline to live their life ethically. Unfortunately, some men and women in the Retail Sector choose to lie, defraud, and steal, in addition to doing much worse. Other men and women just want to deliberate and dispute ideas. However, most men and women in the Retail Sector, who would like to discover an excellent, trustworthy custom of ethical behavior to live their lives by, can discover it in the Golden Rule. Here is exactly why I believe this in all my heart.

This Ethical Compass is Accepted by the Majority of Retail Associates

The likelihood is particularly good that you possess a strong familiarity with exactly how universally recognized the Golden Rule has become. Nevertheless, if you just are not completely convinced, I believe that a powerful case can also be devised for the Golden Rule according to common sense.

Are you able to envision an individual saying, *"Please whatever you do, treat me worse than I treat you, okay?"* Absolutely not going to happen in your lifetime. Every man and woman in Retail desires to be dealt with in a respectful manner. Even men and women who engage in destructive relationships or who happen to participate in detrimental behavior do not really wish or even purposefully seek out poor treatment from other men and women. It is not illogical for any Retail Associate to desire polite treatment from fellow employees. Neither is it asking too much to expect men and women to treat other men and women properly.

It is extremely challenging for a Retail Associate to rationalize the demand for superior treatment from other Retail Associates and customers than they are willing to offer. Exactly what could they base it on? How about employee positions in the store? If that is the situation, the Retail Associate who is part of middle management who wants superior treatment from a Retail Associate at an entry level position would need to consent to being dealt with improperly by those who are in a Senior Management position.

What if Retail Associates based treatment of others on expertise? Or what if Retail Associates based their treatment of others on political affiliation or personally held beliefs?

You can understand exactly where this could certainly end up. Regardless of what haphazard requirements you can imagine, no matter whether its level of position, expertise, ideology, nationality, race, or something else entirely, it simply cannot end up being rationally reinforced. This type of misguided application would become just like a giant game of king of the hill. Perhaps you played that game as a child? One individual ascends upwards on top of the hill and attempts to remain there whilst everyone else attempts to topple them off the top. The only method to win the game is usually to be the biggest bully. And in many cases if you do win the game, you get pummeled along the way.

One of the primary principles in human relationships is to seek out mutual understanding with other men and women. That is an outstanding guideline regardless of whether you are discovering a brand-new relationship, meeting with a perspective customer, coaching a member of your retail team, uniting with your children, or experiencing a spirited discussion with your significant other. Comparing and contrasting related experiences and discovering shared beliefs can pave the way for successful relationships. The

Golden Rule enables you to develop mutual understanding with any other man or woman.

The Ethical Compass is Straightforward as well as Simple to Comprehend

As Retail Associates we quite often have trouble comprehending the subject matter of ethics mainly because it is complicated as well as intangible. One of many wonderful things about the Golden Rule would be that it helps make the abstract discernible. The application is simply not about comprehending the law. It is not a philosophical exercise. You merely visualize yourself in the place of the other person. Even a tiny child can understand that simple concept. There are not any complex protocols and absolutely no escape clauses.

Now it is extremely important to say at this stage that not every ethical situation can be resolved instantaneously by utilizing the Golden Rule. Sometimes the most challenging part of asking, *"How would I like to be treated in this situation?"* is distinguishing who may very well be impacted by the specific situation and what impact it may have on them. However, for even the most sophisticated challenges, if you take the time to give the subject some consideration, you can often figure it out.

With This Ethical Compass Everyone Wins

You have had the displeasure of meeting men and women as a Retail Associate who believe that for them to be those that succeed, other men and women need to be made to lose? I know that I have, and in most cases, you can see them from a mile away. These Retail Associates view absolutely everyone as an adversary who needs to be squashed, or these men and women take advantage of the discomfort of other men and women so that they can succeed.

Could you imagine if your Retail company decided to implement a new compensation package that allowed you to financially benefit from the destruction or weaknesses of fellow employees or customers? Would you consider this to be ethically or morally reprehensible?

Not everyone believes that financial gain from morally reprehensible or socially irresponsible sectors of our society is a terrible thing.

"Whether you have taken a finance class in college or not, most are familiar with this rudimentary lesson: there is a significant difference between a good company versus what makes a company a good investment. In other words, a company's contribution to our society's well-being at the end of the day has little sway over whether or not that business makes for a lucrative investment opportunity."

"We are digging deeper into the age-old debate between good companies versus good investments as we profile 10 stocks that have delivered impressive returns, but also happen to fall under the "bad for your health" category."

1. British American Tobacco
2. McDonald's
3. Coca-Cola Co.
4. Lockheed Martin
5. PepsiCo
6. The Geo Group, Inc.
7. Diageo
8. Wynn Resorts
9. J&J Snack Foods
10. Exxon Mobil

"As an investor, you are bound to encounter instances where your ethics and morals collide with your goals to generate meaningful returns in your portfolio. While it's no easy chore, it's important to separate how you feel about a company and whether or not it's actually a good investment; you might have to put your conscience aside when making some of these decisions, seeing as how some of the most prosperous investments are not necessarily the "healthiest" ones."[xvii]

In a world where the focus always is on one winner and one loser, the philosophy behind the Golden Rule will help ground us and offer a true win-win opportunity.

This Ethical Compass Will Always Point You in The Right Direction

The Golden Rule really does more than merely offer men and women victories. What is more, it possesses inner value for each Retail Associate who chooses to exercise this option. Within a world involving significant ambiguity, I genuinely believe that numerous men and women in the Retail Sector are searching for the right path. The Golden Rule can supply that for you or anyone that you know. The Golden Rule under no circumstances ever changes. It provides sound, foreseeable direction each time it is utilized. And the greatest thing of all, the Golden Rule works.

The "Gold Standard" for Best Places to Work For

Sixteen years ago, Fortune Magazine started a list of the *"100 Best Companies to Work For"* that took into consideration more than just revenue and philanthropic endeavors.

About Our Methodology - Fortune 100 Best Companies to Work For® 2021

People analytics firm Great Place to Work determined the *Fortune 100 Best Companies to Work For™ list* and the *Fortune Best Big Companies to Work For list* by conducting America's largest ongoing annual workforce study, representing more than 4.3 million employees (about twice the population of New Mexico) this year alone.

Employees responded to over 60 survey questions describing the extent to which their organization creates a Great Place to Work for All™. Eighty-five percent of the evaluation is based on what employees' report about their experiences of trust and reaching their full human potential as part of their organization, no matter who they are or what they do. We analyze these experiences relative to each organization's size, workforce make up, and what is typical in their industry and region.

The remaining pieces we consider include an assessment of all employees' daily experiences of the company's values, people's ability to contribute innovative ideas, and the effectiveness of their leaders, to ensure they are consistently experienced.

To be considered, companies would submit an application documenting over 200 datapoints describing their HR (Human Resources) programs and practices. Great Place to Work then conducts a confidential survey of each company's workforce. To ensure surveys truly represent all employees, we require enough people in each organization to respond that results are accurate to a 95% confidence level and 5% margin of error or better. One part of the total score is based on our evaluation of company programs and policies, while three parts come from our analysis of employees' survey data.

They review any anomalies in survey responses, news, and financial performance to ensure there are not any extraordinary reasons to believe they could not trust a company's survey results. Companies need to employ at least 1,000 US (United States) employees to be considered for the 100 Best Companies list, and at least 100,000 US employees to be considered for the Best Big Companies to Work For list. Government agencies are not eligible. [xviii]

This year in 2021, seven of the one hundred Best Companies to Work For are from the Retail Sector. [xix]

- ❖ #3 - **Wegmans Food Markets, Inc.** - What employees are saying - I truly feel that Wegmans is a company where employees can follow the American Dream. We are given endless opportunities to learn and grow. It is a place where those who seek to build a career for themselves while following their passions can do so.
- ❖ #20 - **CarMax** - What employees are saying - The atmosphere here at CarMax is what makes it a great place to work. The people they employ here have great positive mental attitudes and are

constantly encouraging you to do and be better as a person and as an employee.

- ❖ #39 - **Publix Super Markets Inc.** - What employees are saying - Managers tell us thank you at the end of the night and appreciate our work. Customers value our service. The store is safe and clean. Co-workers pitch in and help each other. I feel cared about and supported. I am glad to be here!
- ❖ #60 - **Recreational Equipment, Inc. (REI)** - What employees are saying - There is a sense of a greater purpose and community for those that work here. In meeting other employees and leaders of various levels at headquarters and from around the country I have never encountered anyone that views their work as just a job.
- ❖ #79 - **Nugget Market, Inc.** - What employees are saying - It is the only job that I have had that makes me feel like I am a real contributor to the workplace, not just another worker bee. My hard work is noticed and rewarded both with in-store awards but also through raises and promotions.
- ❖ #80 - **Sheetz, Inc.** - What employees are saying - The connection that upper management has, and the general interest in thoughts and opinions, with all levels

of employment. This is what will continue Sheetz on an upward trajectory.

- ❖ #92 - **Custom Ink** - What employees are saying - This is the first company I have ever worked for where I can tell that each person, all the way up to the Chief Executive Officer, cares. I know I could walk up to any single person, and they would do anything they could to help me personally.

What Are the Different Types of Retail Stores?

Here are some examples of the distinct types of retail stores where consumers can purchase products for immediate use or consumption.

- **Department Stores:** Sell a wide range of merchandise that is arranged by category into different sections of the physical retail space. Some department store categories include shoes, clothing, beauty products, jewelry, housewares, etc. Examples of department store retailers include Macy's, Nordstrom, and JCPenney, to name just a few.
- **Grocery Stores and Supermarkets:** Sell all types of food and beverage products, and sometimes also home products, clothing, and consumer electronics as well.
- **Warehouse Retailers:** Large no-frills warehouse-type facilities stocked with a large variety of products packaged in large quantities and sold at lower-than-retail prices.
- **Specialty Retailers:** Specialize in a specific category of products. Toys 'R' Us, Victoria's Secret, and Nike are examples of specialty retailers.

- **Convenience Retailer:** Usually part of a retail location which sells gasoline primarily, but also sells a limited range of grocery merchandise and auto care products at a premium "*convenience*" price from a brick-and-mortar store.
- **Discount Retailer:** Sell a wide variety of products are often private labeled or generic brands at below-retail prices. Discount retailers like Family Dollar, Dollar General, and Big Lots will often source closeout and discontinued merchandise at lower-than-wholesale prices and pass the savings onto their customers.
- **Mobile Retailer:** Uses a smartphone platform to process retail transactions and then ship the products that were purchased directly to the customer.
- **Internet Retailer:** Sells from an Internet shopping website and ship the purchases directly to customers at their homes or workplaces and without all the expenses of a traditional brick-and-mortar retailer, usually sell merchandise for a lower-than-retail price.

2021 Top 100 Retailers

"Retailing encompasses more today than it ever has before. A year from now it will encompass even more. Whatever the future may hold, the present is still dominated, at least in terms of sales, by retailers with a bricks-and-mortar heritage: Bricks-and-mortar accounts for about 90 percent of total sales.

Stability is reflected in the first 10 positions on STORES Magazine's annual Top 100 Retailers list: The companies are the same as they were last year, with the only changes being six of them moved up or down a notch in swapping positions with each other." xx

1. Walmart
2. Amazon
3. Kroger
4. Home Depot
5. Costco
6. Walgreens
7. Target
8. CVS Health Corporation
9. Lowe's
10. Albertsons

2021 World's Most Ethical Companies

For a generation of Americans that accounts for more than $1 trillion (about $3,100 per person in the US) in consumer spending, buying is more than just a transaction. For Millennials and Generation Z, every purchase is a chance to make a difference.

These young people often choose to support ethical companies that promote transparent and ethical business practices, use sustainable materials, and are aware of their social impact.

While for some brands, ethics equals reducing risks by "doing no harm," other companies have realized an enormous potential in business ethics.

Let us look at some of the world's most ethical companies. [xxi]

1. **3M**
2. **Patagonia**
3. **Kellogg's**
4. **Boden**
5. **John Deere**
6. **Pact**
7. **IBM**
8. **Eileen Fisher**
9. **Allianz Group**
10. **Sézane**

11. PepsiCo
12. ABLE
13. Tradlands
14. Kao
15. Outerknown
16. Tentree
17. Kotn

The Golden Rule is good for Retail Associates because it is a win for everybody. It is great for customers and even investors. The Golden Rule really does work and is the fundamental of ethics.

Observation from a Retail Associate

Just for fun I thought that I would include a list of the 30 of the Worst Things About Working Retail for a chuckle. *You may be surprised how many on the list could be handled with an ethical compass.*

The 30 Worst Things About Working in Retail

1. **Customers Who Keep Shopping Past Closing** - "*No, please continue shopping. I love being here 45 minutes later than I should be because you want to keep looking and then spend $11.*"
2. **Parents Who Let Their Kids Treat the Store Like a Playground** - *These are the type of parents who pretend to be shocked when their kid has an accident that makes the news.*
3. **People** - *10% of customers are great people. The other 90% slowly force you to hate humanity.*
4. **Cleaning the Store** - *Approach endcap, fill, fold, organize by size, watch child throw 45 minutes of work on the floor, repeat.*
5. **Clopen** - *Leaving a closing shift and doing an opening shift the following day.*
6. **Customers Complaining About Price** - *It is a chain store. Not a mom and pop. Their prices are not negotiable. And if they do "hook*

you up," it flags in the system, and they are fired. But hey, you saved $5!

7. **Ringing Register** - *At some point, every employee will face that moment where they have a line of mean muggin' customers and no back up cashier. What makes it even better is every customer who says, "Are you the only one here? Why don't they staff more people?"*

8. **Customers Who Don't Believe Everything is on the Floor** - *If an employee tells you that everything is on the floor, they are usually telling the truth. When you insist, they check anyway, they spend 5 minutes out back trash talking you while pretending to look.*

9. **Customer Says, "It Didn't Scan So It Must Be Free"** - *Every time you must make that fake smirk to avoid awkwardness, a small part of your soul dies.*

10. **Working Holidays** - *It is not a merry or happy anything when you must work.*

11. **Customers Who Expect You to Fetch Their List** - *"Here is my list of things I want. Go fetch!"*

12. **Single Coverage** - *"If I have to pee, who is going to watch for thieves?!"*

13. **Customer Service Program** - *1. Greet every customer within 1 minute. 2. Ask "open-ended questions." 3. Keep eye contact and a smile. 4. Subdue the thoughts of suicide.*

14. **Returns** - *Who the hell buys this much stuff they do not want?!?!?*

15. **District Managers** - *Judging you one day at a time from a morning email of numbers.*
16. **Working Weekends** - *If you want to see a Retail Associate lose their mind, say to them the phrase 'Sunday Funday.'*
17. **Upselling** - *"I see you are buying this $40 item. Can I interest you in this $50 accessory? PLEASE BUY IT OR THEY WILL WRITE ME UP!"*
18. **Secret Shoppers** - *Anyone can sign up to be a "secret shopper" without needing an interview. This person can simply make up the answers to a survey that jeopardizes someone else's job.*
19. **Doubles** - *Working open to close happens more often than you think.*
20. **Morning Shifts Before the Sun Rises** - *There is not enough coffee or Red Bull in the world.*
21. **Customer Holds** - *You know you are not going to go back tomorrow. Why are you making me hold it?*
22. **When You Check A $100 Bill and the Customer Says, "I Just Made That This Morning."** - *HAHAHAHAHAHAHA. Oh man. You could be the funniest person ever.*
23. **Night Shifts** - *Looking out the front window of the store to see people going to enjoy their night while you fix the display some jerk kid knocked over.*

24. **Regional Managers** - *They are thought to be a myth until that once a quarter visit when you crap your pants.*
25. **Inventory** - *Inventory is worse than losing a loved one.*
26. **Conference Calls** - *District Manager: "Why are your sales numbers down?" Store Manager: "Because you make me sit on the phone for hours a day talking to you when I should be on the floor."*
27. **Store Managers** - *Thanks for giving me orders from your throne on wheels.*
28. **Audits** - *Senseless score keeping that is done by requirement. It is dreaded by the store and district manager alike.*
29. **Loss Prevention Managers** - *They have a quota of employees they are expected to catch stealing or making honest mistakes at register and fire.*
30. **Working Hungover** - *90% of the people helping you are hungover. Drinking is the only thing that keeps them from killing you.* [xxii]

"How would I like to be treated in this situation?"

What a great question to be able to ask yourself when you come up against a situation where you are unsure of how to do the "*right*" thing.

Could you imagine if your fellow employees or management used the same question under similar circumstances?

Once you have answered this question, I recommend asking the next question:

"What could I do, so that I give back more than I would wish to receive in this situation?"

Always looking to give back more is another strong relationship builder.

The adoption of the *"Golden Rule"* for you and your store is an easy decision!

It is accepted by everyone, easily understood by everyone, poses a win-win philosophy, and will help you navigate through just about any situation.

Why the Ethical "*Gold Standard*" Begins with You

Over the past few years, the entire world has been struggling to overcome a monetary crisis because of numerous deficit problems. One of these deficit problems which happen to be highly relevant to this book is the significant deficit of leadership.

When we consider the United States of America as an example, the deficit of leadership has not been more obvious as compared to any other time in history.

Why is it that the United States seems to be developing less capable leadership?

The problem can be traced back to the United States education system.

Back in the day when the U.S (United States). Founding Fathers were being raised, 90% of the educational push was of a moral, ethical, and religious nature.

Fast forward to the late 1950's the percentage of that same educational push was so tiny it could not end up being effectively measured.

If we were to look back at the U.S. in 1776, the population was somewhere around three million people, and yet such legendary leaders as

Washington, Madison, Jefferson, Hamilton, Adams, etc.., were created.

Jump ahead to today and the U.S. does not have anyone equal to the men of that caliber with a population of 329,316,857+. These same problems exist in many countries around the world. [xxiii]

A solid ethical education empowers an individual to help to make superior ethical decisions. Nevertheless, because very few people today have obtained such an educational framework, how is it possible to get started on the correct ethical path? Just how do you take something as extensive as the Golden Rule and then make it an integral part of your day-to-day ethical thinking?

A sensible way to begin would be to consider exactly what our needs as humans are.

Therefore, why don't we begin with discussing precisely what causes men and women to end up being fulfilled and just what leads to us not being fulfilled. We need to understand the distinction between influence and drive.

Regardless of what we choose to do in everyday life, it comes with an emotional side to everything you and I do.

Many of us make a big effort to disregard this, simply because we are attempting to get the task completed. However, it is the component that not only fulfills all of us but fuels all of us as men and women. And unless you understand or know that fuel, unless you recognize that drive, then you will continually be seeking to get a temporary burst of energy by means of self-discipline or concentration, however you would never be in a place to just flow.

Where it simply occurs. Where it is simply automatic.

Let us drill down a bit deeper on this subject matter.

All human beings possess diverse desires; however, we are all motivated by the exact same set of needs. Understanding the six human needs makes it possible for you to turn on your internal motivator, discover all you are capable of, and be genuinely fulfilled regularly. But before we discuss those six needs, let us look at a way of categorizing our experiences.

Human Experience – The Four Classes xxiv

1. Most people typically consider a Class One experience as a *"peak life experience."* A Class One experience:
   a. Feels very good,
   b. It is very good for you,
   c. It is very good for others,
   d. Will serve the greater good.
2. Most men and women desire to avoid Class two experiences. Understanding their concepts, however, leads us to the most pleasure, development, and fulfillment. The Class Two experience:
   a. Does not feel very good,
   b. It is very good for you,
   c. It is very good for others,
   d. Will serve the greater good.
3. Non-productive Class Three experiences tend to provide instant enjoyment; however, at some point they damage our own standard of living and supply us with the greatest pain. Drinking alcohol to excess would most definitely fit into this category. Class Three experience:
   a. Feels very good,
   b. It is not very good for you,
   c. It is not very good for others, and
   d. Genuinely does not serve the greater good.

4. Men and women frequently take pleasure in Class Four experiences because of pressure from peers, conditioning, or perhaps outdated belief systems. Cigarette smoking, as an example, typically does not feel good the very first time, however, many men and women continue doing it. The Class Four experience is something that:
    a. Genuinely does not feel very good,
    b. It is not very good for you,
    c. It is not very good for others, and
    d. Does not serve the greater good.

Let me explain to you what I consider the key to a successful, happy, and fulfilling life. It is discovering how to transform Class Two Experiences directly into Class One Experiences. Discovering how to take those experiences that don't really feel very good, however, are really very good for you, truly serve others, are very good for others and truly serve the greater good and make the Class One experience where it also feels very good for you.

Do you believe that if you possessed the capability to survey every person on the planet, that the survey would likely reveal that men and women around the world possess comparable problems?

Yet each one of these men and women reside in various areas of the world and possess diverse belief systems. You will discover diverse rules. They all would have diverse backgrounds and different experiences. Exactly how could they possibly have similar problems?

Is it feasible that all human beings have the same needs?

Okay, as crazy as it sounds, it may be possible. So why would they have the same problems?

Is it feasible that these needs are basically in turmoil and that is the reason we have the challenge? Would God do this to us? No, it might help to make life much more intriguing, almost certainly help to make us need to grow more, most likely help to make us attempt to figure things out.

The Six Human Needs

All men and women possess the same problems due to the fact everyone has the same six human needs. These needs are generally peculiar, in that they are most often in conflict. Serious problems can occur whenever we select harmful tools or vehicles to attempt to fulfill these needs. As an alternative, we can decide to set up brand new behaviors for fulfilling our needs which will shift us swiftly toward life mastery.[xxv]

To be fulfilled, we must consistently meet these six human needs:

- Certainty/Comfort
- Uncertainty/Variety
- Significance
- Connection/Love
- Growth
- Contribution

All human beings have the need for:

1. **Certainty/Comfort**
    a. For most people, certainty equates to them surviving. We all require certainty that the roof will hold over our heads, the floor holds underneath our feet, and that we can avoid discomfort and acquire enjoyment.

b. Precisely how do we satisfy this requirement for certainty? Quite a few men and women try to achieve it by grabbing items that cause them to become certain they can be comfortable: food, drugs, alcohol, or cigarettes. Other individuals find it by submerging themselves in their work or by attempting to control every little thing around them, their environment, or other people. These situations are usually Class Three experiences [they may feel good for the moment but are not good for you, not good for those around you, and do not serve the greater good.]
c. Exactly how do you attempt to get certainty in your life? Eliminate a few of the ways you attempt to be certain you can be comfortable, steer clear of discomfort, and acquire enjoyment.
d. Here is the contradiction, though. Whenever you feel completely certain, when situations are totally predictable, you satisfy this need and become bored. And so, although we would like certainty,

we concurrently would like a certain amount of...

2. **Uncertainty/Variety**
    a. Absolutely everyone needs variety, something unexpected, and a challenge to really feel completely alive as well as experience fulfillment. With an excessive amount of certainty, we are bored. Similarly, together with too much variety, we turn out to be very afraid and concerned.
    b. Men and women will certainly breach their values in order to meet their needs. Selecting unacceptable vehicles only results in discomfort.
    c. There is a fragile balance between both needs that really must be struck for all of us to really feel truly fulfilled. Most people need a level of certainty within their lives to fully appreciate the variety. Several men and women choose destructive methods for getting variety, such as using drugs or alcohol to alter their emotional states or the way they feel. Other individuals select neutral vehicles, like watching movies. Still others use constructive vehicles, like

stimulating dialogue and opportunities to learn.
    d. How do you try to get variety in your life? List some of the constructive ways you try to create surprises, challenges, and diversity in your life.

3. **Significance**
    a. We all have a need for significance, the sense that we are distinctive in some manner, that our lives possess a special purpose or meaning. We can try to satisfy this need through detrimental vehicles, for example, making ourselves unique by manufacturing and believing that we are better than everyone else or by developing extreme problems that set us apart. Medical science research has shown that some men and women have even created the subconscious capability to make themselves sick so that they can gain the nurturing consideration of other individuals. This would clearly be a Class Four experience.
    b. Some men and women create a uniqueness by simply earning more income, possessing more

"*toys*," attending school and achieving more degrees, or dressing in a distinctive way and possessing a fashion sense. Quite a few decide to live lives of incredible service to others, a positive Class One experience that could feel as if it was Class Two from time to time.

c. Just how do you attempt to obtain significance in your life? List some of the things you do that cause you to feel distinctive, needed, satisfied, or significant.

d. We all need to feel unique. However paradoxically, in order to really feel unique, we must separate ourselves from other people. If we were feeling completely unique, we feel different and separate, which violates our need for...

4. **Connections/Love**
    a. All men and women need to feel connected with themselves, as well as with others with whom they can share their love.
    b. In order to satisfy this need, you can join a group or a club that possesses a positive purpose. Several people join gangs, which have negative applications but

still provide that sense of connection. Quite a few people feel immediate connection by aligning with their creator and feeling like they are being guided. People will steal, take drugs, or drink excessive amounts of alcohol to be part of the group and feel a sense of connection. Other individuals will perform at an extraordinary level to be accepted, loved, or connected to a high-performance team.

c. As with all six human needs, I you give consistently that which you wish to receive, you will end to get it back from others.

d. How do you try to get connection and love in your life? List some of the ways you try to feel connected to yourself, others, to your creator.

e. These first four needs are basic needs. The next two would be primary needs that must be met for you to feel totally fulfilled as a person.

5. **Growth**

a. Growth equals life. On this planet, everything that is alive is either growing or dying. It does not matter how much money you have; how many people acknowledge you, or what you have achieved... Unless you feel like you are growing, you will be unhappy and unfulfilled. But you must also be able to experience the euphoria of meaningful...

6. **Contribution**
   a. We all have a deep need to go beyond ourselves and to live a life that serves the greater good. In the moments that we do this, we experience true joy and fulfillment.
   b. Contributing not only to others but to ourselves is a meaningful action, for we cannot give to others that what we do not have. A balance of contributions to oneself and to others, especially unselfish contributions, is the ultimate secret to the joy that so many people wish to have in their lives.
   c. How do you try to get growth and contribution in your life? List some of the things you do to obtain the feeling that you are growing and contributing, to yourself, to others, to the world at large.

The Reason Why Most People Love or Hate to Try and Do Things

Therefore, if these are generally our six human needs, if these are generally our goals, then what exactly have we discovered? Here is what we discovered. To begin with, you can satisfy these first four needs in detrimental approaches and therefore will feel somewhat satisfied. Enough that you will not be happy, but you will not be discontented enough to change. And you will probably not be satisfied simply because you will not grow and contribute, which are the supreme, fundamental, crucial needs.

This means that, for example, you have access to certainty in your life simply by controlling everybody. And on a zero to ten scale, perhaps that feels like Level 3 of enjoyment and satisfaction. Are you with me so far? After which if you go to significance, chances are you will do it by way of tearing everybody else down, consequently making yourself feel more significant.

That behavior may provide you with a Level 3 or a 4. And you could have connection and love by receiving compassion on a regular basis, or being demanding, and observing that men and women are generally responding to you and then calling that love, which we know deep down it is not. These methods will not help you to grow, they are not going to trigger you to contribute, and therefore you will not be satisfied. This is a frightening place in life. When you are performing everything, you believe you are designed to do it and you are accomplishing it all, and you are still not satisfied. Now you will know why.

Do you get it? Boy, if you just find a few vehicles, a few of them that meet all your needs, you cannot believe it. You will not need to inspire yourself. You will not really need to get yourself venturing out there. You will not really need to give yourself a little push and listen to your little pump-up CD's. You can listen to compact discs to get educated, listen to compact discs to get entertained, maybe just to remind yourself of the issues. But you will know what to do because the drive will be inside you.

And you know what? You already possess this in certain areas of your life. Consider it. Where is there an area in your life where there is something, you love to do that for you is effortless? I would be willing to bet that no less than four of these six human needs are satisfied with that activity, and in all probability all six.

What is Something You Absolutely Hate to Do?

Prior to answering the above-mentioned question, think about something you love to do and ask yourself, on a scale from zero to ten, how satisfied am I by that with regards to just how much certainty I experience feeling? When I contemplate doing that, just how much certainty do I have that I will have enjoyment performing that task? Just how much certainty do I have that I will have fun with it, that I will have ease and comfort at the very least? At a minimum, you can avoid discomfort.

And then go to variety. How much uncertainty, how much variety on a scale of zero to ten will I have by participating? How much is different? How much of this would make me feel significant, unique, or needed? And how much of this will give me these feelings of connection and love? How much of this will give me growth on a zero to ten scale? Contribution? And again, if it is something you lo to do, I promise you, under your current strategy for perceiving things, appreciating them, noticing them; under your current strategy for doing things, you feel fulfilled in all six categories.

Now recall something you absolutely hate to try and do. What is something you attempt to avoid carrying out if you can? Some of you will say, *"Cleaning my house."*

Okay, so on a scale of zero to ten; what is your degree of certainty that will provide you with enjoyment or relaxation? Something like negative two. To some people it is a complete waste of time. Most people absolutely hate cleaning their house. To some people it makes them uncomfortable because they are wasting time, and other things they could be doing are not getting done because of it.

What is your own sense of variety in cleaning your house, on a scale of zero to ten? To some people it would still be a negative two. They feel there is absolutely no variety in cleaning. It's the same house, the same crap; it is in the same place. It is boring.

What is your sense of significance cleaning your house? Significance? To some people there is no significance, so on a scale of zero to ten, it would be zero.

How about connection and love? To some people it would be zero.

Let us look at growth. These same people would say zero.

Lastly, how about contribution? Simple, zero.

It is not necessarily too difficult to figure out. But guess what? There are men and women, hat if asked, "*Who here loves to clean their house?*" Several men and women will raise their hands and say they love to clean their house. And do you know why that is great? Because we all want to hire them, right?

So, if these men and women were asked, *"Do you have a sense of certainty that you're going to have enjoyment when you clean your house?"* Their response may be, *"Absolutely, because you know what? When everything else in my life is so stirred up, I go clean my house. I feel like I've control over it, I feel good about things, I feel happy. You know, part of it is I have time for myself. And I know I do an excellent job. And I am certain I can do an excellent job. And can complete it and get it done."*

Let us ask these men and women, *"Do you have a sense of variety from cleaning the house?"* The response may be, *"Well, of course I do. Every time you clean the house, you don't know what you are going to find. Your kids put something down where it does not belong. There is always something new in various places. Plus, I often listen to CD's, so I am hearing something different I am learning something while I am cleaning."*

How about significance, *"Do you get significance from cleaning your house?"* They may answer, *"Yes, I do, because I do a better job than anybody else."*

How about connection and love, *"Do you get connection and love from cleaning your house?"* The response may be, *"Yes, I do, because when I'm ironing, I pray for my children, and I feel connected to them."*

How about growth, *"Do you really grow when you are cleaning the house?"* You may hear something like, *"Yes, because I listen to CD's, I think about different ideas, I ask myself questions. Plus, I solve recent problems in the house, new challenges. Of course, I am growing."*

How about contribution, *"Do you get a feeling of contribution from cleaning your house?"* You may be surprised and hear, *"Absolutely, nobody else will do it, so I am contributing. That also makes me unique because no one else will do it."*

Now let us connect all this. I will provide you with a few good examples after which let us connect it to you. But to start with, think for just a moment. What is the one thing you absolutely hate to do? With that thought of wat you absolutely hate to do in your mind, ask yourself, *"This one thing I hate to do or to be politically correct, I'd prefer other people to do, what's my degree of certainty that I'll have enjoyment or at least avoid discomfort by doing this, that I will be comfortable doing this?"* Zero to ten, precisely what is your degree of certainty it will be enjoyable? I would be inclined to wager it is low, isn't it? It is zero, possibly below? Then again, it is two, three or four.

Precisely what is your sense of positive variety on a zero to ten scale? That there will be positive surprises or differences in this activity? One of the reasons you don't like doing it is you don't see there is variety. To you it is the same old thing. Some other people enjoy it because they see variety in it, but you do not. Zero to ten? Yes, you are in that minus level, one, two, in that range. Right?

Consider significance? This specific thing you hate to do. Exactly how significant does it make you feel? How important do you feel? How unique do you feel while you are doing this? My guess is low or zero.

What about the sense of connection and love when you do it? Consider it for a moment. How connected? How much love do you experience doing this thing you hate to do? My guess is pretty darn low again.

How about growth? You might go, *"Yeah, I grow when I am doing it."* No. I don't mean you grow. I said when you think about doing it, how much growth do you associate with it? Truly little.

And again, contribution? You answer, *"Yeah, I contribute."* Again, I don't want to know if you contribute. I want to know how does it feels when you think about doing this; do you feel like you are contributing? Now many times you do contribute but you don't give yourself credit so that is why it does not feel fulfilling.

Does this make sense to you? Anything in life can be totally fulfilling if you know what the goal of the game is. All you need to do is organize the game to meet it.

So, now you are a little more aware of how we classify our experiences, as well as the depth of the six human needs.

Now with this knowledge of the six human "macro" needs, let us focus our attention on the Retail Associate and their "*micro*" needs...

Adopting the Ethical "Gold Standard"

Exactly how should we as Retail Associates commence the adoption of this Ethical Guideline?

Just how do you take something as wide-ranging as the Golden Rule and help to make it an integral part of your day-to-day thinking?

Begin with this question:

How would I, as a Retail Associate, want to be treated?

I have faith that all Retail Associates, at their core, are very much alike.

Below is a condensed list of things which I believe that all men and women share with regards to the way they wish to be treated:

As a Retail Associate, I Truly Would Like to be Valued

Are you aware that within the United States Economic marketplace over the past 20+ years, over 70% of men and women leave their day jobs and do so because they do not feel valued by their employer. [xxvi]

What percentage of these men and women are part of the Retail Sector?

Let us run some quick numbers. The population of the United States at the printing of this book was 329,386,235. [xxvii]

So, 70% of the population would equal 230,570,364.

What if only 10% of the 70% (230,570,364) were part of the Retail Sector, how many fellow Retail Associates are impacted with the feeling of being undervalued?

Answer: 23,057,036+ men and women.

There is not a Retail Associate in the world that does not desire to be valued by others. Wouldn't you desire other individuals to simply accept you for who you really are and demonstrate through their daily actions that you matter and make a difference?

Most people have experienced the feeling of being worthless because of another person's actions. See if the list below reminds you of anyone.

A schoolteacher or even a whole lot worse a parent or guardian who informed you that you as an individual have absolutely nothing to offer this world.

Your employer or supervisor announced that you and your division are really a financial drain on the company.

Some individual made the decision that it would most likely end up being amusing or publicly humiliating to you.

If any one of the three hits home, then you already know precisely how essential it is to be valued by another human being.

In the Retail Sector, inspiration is like oxygen; it is far better to have it than not to have it.

I am of the belief that deep down, about all Retail Associates desire to feel that they matter simply for who they are.

This is basically the idea regarding the valuing of others. The cornerstone of the Golden Rule is to value others for who they are as human beings and not what they can do for us or what position they may hold in the real world.

If you truly understand this concept, then you are well on your way to making the Golde Rule your ethical compass.

As a Retail Associate, I Truly Wish to be Appreciated

The desire to end up being cherished and valued could very well be the number one need of every Retail Associate.

The second greatest need would most likely be our desire to be appreciated for our effort and hard work. Most Retail Associates possess the desire to succeed and accomplish great things.

It is fair to say that you want to be appreciated for the expertise and hard work you bring to your organization and personal life. So, if you happen to all be like me, it is especially important to recognize that what you do matters in the larger scheme of things and helps develop your self-confidence and personal self-worth.

Why compare yourself with others? No one in the entire world can do a better job of being you than you.

Here are four ways to start the process of appreciation:

1. Start by trying to communicate to other Retail Associates that you personally appreciate their efforts.
2. Say thanks to them at each chance.
3. Offer credit to others whenever you can

4. Make a point to praise Retail Associates in the presence of those closest to them, such as other Retail Associates or family.

As a Retail Associate I Truly Wish to be Trusted

It could very well be said that trust is the foundation of all good relationships. Whether it is marriage, business relationships, or a friendship, all require trust. If you don't have trust, there can never be any open or honest interaction, and most likely that relationship will be only temporary.

The list below contains some of the best ways that a Retail Associate can build trust with others:

- Display compassion on a consistent basis.
- Preserve your own integrity.
- Retain those things that you hold in confidence from others.
- Concentrate upon mutual objectives as opposed to personal itineraries.
- Always listen with an open mind.
- Demonstrate respect for your fellow workers, your customers, or equivalent.
- Carry out what is right, irrespective of personal risk.
- Freely and honestly communicate vision and values.

"A good marriage is at least 80 percent good luck in finding the right person at the right time. The rest is trust."
- Nanette Newman

It is going to take a leap of faith to place your trust in another individual, especially someone you don't know very well. Nevertheless, that is what must be done to put into practice the Golden Rule. Ironically, nurturing a new Retail Associate requires a similar leap of faith on your part.

As a Retail Associate, I Truly Wish to be Respected

Anytime that another person places trust in you, you acquire accountability as well as recognition. Whenever others respect you, it will touch something much deep within you. This trust placed in you will provide you with dignity and will help build your self-confidence.

"Thought cannot avoid the ethical or reverence and love for all life. It will abandon the old confined systems of ethics and be forced to recognize that ethics that knows no bounds. But on the other hand, those who believe in love for all creation must realize clearly the difficulties involved in the problem of boundless ethic and must be resolved not to veil from [humankind] the conflicts, which this ethic will involve [us], but allow [us] really to experience them. To think out in every implication the ethic of love for all creation – this is the difficult task, which confronts our age." - Albert Schweitzer

10 Rules for Respect

1. If you have a problem with me, come to me (privately).
2. If I have a problem with you, I will come to you (privately).
3. If someone has a problem with me and comes to you, send them to me. (I will do the same for you.)
4. If someone consistently will not come to me, say, "*Let us go to them together. I am sure they will see us about this.*" (I will do the same for you.)
5. Be careful how you interpret me – I would rather do that. In matters that are unclear, I do not feel pressured to interpret my feelings or thoughts. It is easy to misinterpret intentions.
6. I will be careful how I interpret you.
7. If it is confidential, don't tell. (This especially applies to business meetings.) If you or anyone comes to me in confidence, I will not tell unless
    a. The person is going to harm himself/herself,
    b. The person is going to physically harm someone else,
    c. A child has been physically or sexually abused. I expect the same from you.
8. I do not read unsigned letters or notes.

9. I do not manipulate; I will not be manipulated; do not let others manipulate you. Do not let others try to manipulate me through you. I will not preach *"at"* you on Sunday mornings. will leave conviction to the Holy Spirit (he does it better anyway.).
10. When in doubt, just say it. The only dumb questions are those that don't get asked. We are family here and we care about each other, so if you have a concern, pray, and then (if led) speak up. If I can answer it without misrepresenting something or breaking confidence, I will. [xxviii]

As a Retail Associate, I Wish to be Understood

At times, a Retail Associate's issue is brought on by yet another individual's callousness or perhaps indifference. However, by and large, the difficulty develops from a lack of knowledge. It is humorous the way we can be fast to find fault with other people when they don't adjust to the behavior or criteria we hold. However, when we take the time to get to know them, we quite often realize that their approach is not the wrong way, it is just a different way.

When dealing with other individuals, we as Retail Associates should seek first to understand, then to be understood. That requires a mindset of overall flexibility along with a desire to be teachable.

I have heard it be said that love is saying, *"I feel differently"* instead of *"your wrong."*

As a Retail Associate, I Truly Do Not Want Others to Take Advantage of Me

About how others treat me, more than anything else, I don't want anyone to take advantage of me. That is the main point here regarding ethical behavior. Most of us don't have to straighten out complex philosophical challenges or ethical riddles. If men and women could decipher that I am taking advantage of them then my actions are in all probability an awful idea.

There exists a revealing account about Marvin Bower, the renowned leader of McKinsey & Co. Who died on January 22, 2003, at age ninety-nine. The story affirms a lot concerning the foundational values of this humble man, who was simply referred to as the father of management consulting.

In the 1950's, Bower was requested to visit Los Angeles by then billionaire Howard Hughes, who wanted him to analyze Paramount Pictures.

Throughout the visit Hughes was in a benevolent disposition and drove the new consultant around in his ancient Chevrolet, even offering him a late-night tour of the Spruce Goose, the enormous wooden plane Hughes developed during the war.

However, Bower believed that absolutely nothing good could possibly come of working for Hughes. He found the entrepreneur's method of business "*so unorthodox and so unusual*" that he believed he would never be able to help Paramount. Instead of taking the assignment and reaping a big fee, he walked away.

The move ended up being classic Bower. He built McKinsey into a global consulting powerhouse by making it mandatory that values mattered more than money. He extolled the idea that consulting was not a business but a profession, arguing that, like the best doctors and lawyers, consultants should put the interests of their clients first, conduct themselves ethically, and insist on telling clients the truth, not what they wanted to hear.

That was as unusual then as it is today. But so was Bower, a towering figure at McKinsey and in the larger world of consulting. At McKinsey, Bower helped to move consulting from shop-floor efficiency studies to major strategy reviews for top-tier corporations. He created one of the world's most productive leadership factories, producing hundreds of corporate CEOs and presidents. [xxix]

Understanding the Value of People

Several companies in the United States are relearning this lesson. They are rediscovering the value of valuing people. Plus, they are generating internal corporate changes to help market the effective treatment of their employees in the marketplace. One company is Starbucks. So, what makes Starbucks so great? Partners at the coffee seller told us, *"I love that we can receive benefits and stock rewards a 20 hours/week"* and *"There is potential for anyone to move up the ladder."* [xxx]

Successful organizations place men and women first, invest in their development and provide them with the tools, training and support they need to be successful. This results not just in bottom line success, but lower attrition rates and higher levels of creativeness, innovation, and excellence.

Here is a list of 30 companies that put employees front and center. They are Google, Quicken Loans, VMware, Arthrex, NuStar Energy, Robert W. Baird, David Weekely Homes, CHG Healthcare Services, Edward Jones, Stryker, Worldwide Technology, Hyatt Hotels, Hyland (creator of Onbase), Novo Nordisk, Alston & Bird, W.L. Gore & Associates, Cadence, Deloitte, American Fidelity Assurance Company, Perkins Coie, KPMG, Baker Donelson, Mars, O.C.

Tanner, Orrick Herrington & Sutcliffe, Texas Health Resources, Goldman Sachs, Cooley, Ultimate Software and SalesForce. [xxxi]

Evidence demonstrates that successful organizations put men and women first. Personnel are a company's only genuine competitive advantage. Competitors can match up with most organizations' products, processes, locations, distribution channels and so on.

Precisely what methods distinguish people-first organizations? An organization that is culturally diverse, family-friendly, invests I employee training and empowers their employees.

Consequently, this converts into higher employee efficiency and fulfilment. These employees are prepared to put forth the extra effort to carry out whatever is necessary to see that their jobs are done properly and completely.

People-first strategies also lead to organizations being able to recruit smarter, more conscientious, and more loyal employees.

7 Reasons Why a People-First Culture is Changing How Leaders Manage Employees

It has been found that people who were happier at work were 12% more productive than those who were unhappy. Take Google as an example, they have invested more in employee support, and employee satisfaction has risen as a result. For Google, it rose by 37%, they know what they are talking about.

This is what a "*people-first*" culture is all about. More and more companies understand that in order to attract and retain employees, they must treat them the same way they would treat their customers. Here are 7 reasons why a people-first culture is winning: [xxxii]

1. Employees Are More Loyal

2. Companies Attract Top Talent More Easily

3. Employees Perform Better

4. Businesses Stay Competitive

5. You Meet Goals Faster

6. You'll Have Better Retention

7. They Have Greater Collaboration

Observations from a Retail Associate

How can you implement the Golden Rule?

You first must take your eyes off yourself, permanently, and focus on what is right for others!

When we are building our department, store, or company, we must ensure that the Retail Associates that join us feel that they are a valued asset to our organization.

How can we do that? There are several ways, but continually communicating with them about their success and that of the store and that you are there to help them achieve what they define as success will go a long way towards making them feel valued.

The same goes for feeling appreciated. We all want to feel appreciated.

Respect is easy when you use the Golden Rule. Everyone deserves to be respected as human beings.

End of story.

How to Live the Ethical "*Gold Standard*" at the Highest Level

It is only a man or woman of character who can influence others. Character is paramount to living a lifetime of integrity and ethical excellence.

As a Retail Associate, Character is Much More Than Speaking

A lot of Retail Associates speak about carrying out what's right, however, action is the true measure of character.

"If you will think about what you ought to do for other people, our character will take care of itself. Character is a by-product, and any man who devotes himself to its cultivation in his own case will become a selfish prig." - Woodrow Wilson

As a Retail Associate, Talent is Really a Gift – Character is Really a Decision

There are plenty of things in life you don't get to select, such as where you are born, who your parents are, and how tall you are. But there are some critical things every person does select. We select our faith, our attitude, and our character.

As a Retail Associate, Character Delivers Long Lasting Achievement

Trust is vital when working with people. Character begets trust.

As a Retail Associate, you are Unable to Exceed the Restrictions of Your Character

There are only three kinds of Retail Associates:

1. Retail Associates who never succeed.
2. Retail Associates who achieve success only temporarily; and
3. Retail Associates who become and remain successful.

Possessing character is the only sure way to sustain success. Regardless of how skilled or attractive a Retail Associate is, they are not going to have the ability to outrun their character.

If you wish to live a character filled life which demonstrates ethical superiority, follow these guidelines. They will assist you to incorporate the Golden Rule into the essence of your life:

1. **Embrace This Guideline as the Integrity Compass for Your Life**
    a. Nobody wants to end up being an echo, to live a shadow of a life. However, that is frequently the destiny of men and women without beliefs. In the event you want your life to have meaning, then you must select some basic principles to live by.

b. Previously I have made the case for the Golden Rule. As I have said, asking the question, *"How would I like to be treated in this situation?"* is an excellent integrity guideline for any situation. It works in your store and in your home. It works with family and friends. It works whether you are leading a department of a few people or an organization of tens of thousands.
c. If you believe the Golden Rule is right and it works, then you need to adopt it as the integrity compass for your life. Every single day, whenever the matter of ethical conduct comes up with you, ask this question: *"How would I like to be treated in this situation?"*
d. By keeping genuine, do not be embarrassed about carrying out the right thing, and choose what you believe is correct and stay with it.

2. **Make Your Choices According to This Integrity Guideline**
   a. Most people make only a couple of critical decisions in life and from that point manage those decisions daily. As soon as you choose to make the Golden Rule

the integrity guideline for your life, you might want to reconsider some of your previous decisions. Such as:
- i. Exactly how will the Golden Rule alter my goals?
- ii. Will I interact differently with my family?
- iii. Will I need to alter the way I approach my career? (Some Retail Associates feel obligated to change jobs because their work environment is averse to Golden Rule Living.)

b. Remember, the more substantial the decision, the greater the courage it could require.

c. Carrying out what is right when it is uncomfortable to do so is no minor thing. However, the benefits are enormous.

d. While you apply the Golden Rule to your life and make decisions based on it, keep in mind the following:
- i. **Choices, and Certainty Not Circumstances, Determine Your Own Integrity**: men and

women of weak character tend to blame their choices on conditions. People of ethics make good choices irrespective of conditions. If they make sufficiently good choices, they start to create much better circumstances for themselves.

ii. **Incorrect Decisions Leave Behind Emotional Disfigurements**: each time men and women make incorrect decisions, there is an impact, regardless of whether they immediately recognize it or not.

iii. **The Greater Amount of People Included, The Greater the Stress about Complying**: moral choices made in private have their own stress, simply because some people might be inclined to believe that a private indiscretion will not ever turn out to be public knowledge. Public decisions connected with other men and women possess a different kind of tress, that of complying. No matter how much stress there is, you simply cannot permit other individuals to pressure you into creating unethical decisions.

iv. **Idleness is Also a Choice**: Some men and women's response to ethical decision-making is to steer clear of acting. Nevertheless, it is essential to keep in mind that idleness is also a decision. Unfortunately, for everyone individual willing to stand-up and point out their companies' ethical transgressions, there are millions of men and women who decide every single day not to act when they observe their companies take shortcuts or compromise

ethics, and to inevitably live with the consequences.
v. To live a life of integrity and ethics, you will need to maintain your principles while you make tough decisions.
vi. Basic principles, especially moral principles, can never be at the mercy of the wind. A moral principle is a compass forever fastened and forever true, and that is as essential in your business as it is in your home.

3. **Control Your Choices in Accordance with this Particular Integrity Guideline**
    a. With regards to ethics, at times it is easy to make substantial decisions. Most people don't have an extremely demanding time making the conscious decision not to take someone's life. A handful of men and women are inclined to perform *"grand theft auto"* or *"breaking and entering."* Nevertheless, minor things can be difficult to control.

There is an old saying, "*god is in the details.*" You can also say that ethics is in the details.

    b. You will discover three primary questions for ethical decision-making:
- i. Is what I am about to do legal?
- ii. Is what I am about to do balanced?
- iii. How will what I am about to do make me feel about myself?

    c. To generally be considered trustworthy, you need to be predictable. When you control your life and all the decisions (minor or major) by a single principle, the Golden Rule, you develop an ethical predictability in your own life. Men and women are going to have confidence in you, understanding that you consistently do the right thing.

4. **Request Other Individuals to Hold You Accountable for Your Actions**

    a. Has another man or woman at any time stood looking over your shoulder while you labored on a task? If that is the case, the chances are fairly good that you did not enjoy it. Most men and women do not appreciate being micromanaged. In addition to being micromanaged for everyday tasks, men and women appreciate it even less when another person checks up on them to make certain that they are being truthful and dependable. Nevertheless, it is precisely what I would recommend that you do if you would like to live by the Golden Rule, simply because absolutely nothing assists a person to be honest like accountability.

b. It really is interesting. Most people don't especially like to be reminded of their own weak points, and we don't especially like our weak points revealed to others either. However, if we want to grow, we will need to deal with the pain of disclosing our own actions to others. Integrity is the foundation of a person's life, and accountability is the cornerstone. It provides teeth to our commitment to live by high ethical standards.

The Golden Rule and the Life of J.C. Penney

Anytime you study the lives of great men and women, you can tell any time one of these *"special people"* has lived their life based on the Golden Rule. Among my favorites is the story of J.C. Penney, the founding father of the department stores that display his name. The son of a farmer, James Cash (J.C.) Penney was raised in Hamilton, Missouri. His father started developing J.C. Penney character early on, teaching him about the marketplace, self-sufficiency, and the Golden Rule. An interesting example of this started when J.C. Penney was 8 years old, he was expected to earn enough money to purchase his own clothes.

To earn money, J.C. Penney labored and scraped together $2.50 to buy a young piglet. Subsequently, he performed house chores for the surrounding neighbors so he could gather slop for the piglet to fatten it up. When J.C Penney sold it during slaughter season, he earned a good profit. Observing the key benefits of such an arrangement, he bought a dozen piglets the next season, and he gathered corn from the farm's rows after the huskers had finished harvesting. The pigs were growing nicely, and J.C. Penney expected to make a great profit in the fall. However, one day his father forced him to sell them simply because the neighbors were protesting and complaining about the smell. J.C. Penney commented, *"It was the off-season for pork... But my father lived by the Golden Rule in relation to his neighbors, and it was important to him for me to see that I should too."* xxxiii

As J.C. Penney got older, he discovered that he had a talent for purchasing and selling, and he constantly labored at it. At the same time, his father encouraged him and made sure he was always honest. He also assisted his son to get his first job in a dry goods store in Hamilton, Missouri. There J.C. Penney learned his trade. In time he managed to move on to other stores, always working hard and treating others as he wanted to be treated. At one store, when he learned that the same socks were priced several different ways in order to take advantage of unwitting customers, he resigned. Eventually he got on with a store whose owners invited him to become a partner. He was so good at his trade; the men offered him a partnership in additional stores they intended to open. And when the original owners wanted to leave the business in 1907, J.C. Penney bought them out.

J.C. Penney had a vision for a chain of stores across the western United States. His strategy was to discover trustworthy, diligent men and teach them his approach to business. And in t event that they succeeded in managing their store well and turned around and trained another man to do the same, he would offer them partnership in a new store, just as it had been offered to him. "*I think, if we pick the right kind of men and train them the right way, they will all catch the spirit of partnership idea."* He told the first manager he invited to become part owner of the store. [xxxiv]

And what were those original stores called? He named them for his philosophy of business. They were called the Golden Rule Stores, *"hence,"* explained J.C. Penney, *"in setting up a business under the name and meaning? Of the Golden Rule, I was publicly binding myself, in my business relations, on a principle which had been a real and intimate part of my family upbringing. To me the sign in the store was much more than the trade name."* [xxxv]

Though J.C. Penney later changed the names of the stores when his organization incorporated during expansion, he never stopped living, and working, by the Golden Rule, putting partnership ahead of profits. He stated his philosophy succinctly: *"money is properly the by-product of building men as partners."* [xxxvi]

J.C. Penney continued to work and create partners for many years. He finally turned the business over to one of the people he had made a partner, a man who had worked for him in one of the fir stores. J.C. Penney lived by the Golden Rule, treating others with respect, giving them value in business, and providing the best merchandise he could procure. He lived to be 95 years old.

There is a classic saying that when you get squeezed, whatever is in you will come out. That makes sense and that is true. However, I also understand that an individual is unable to develop a Golden Rule life overnight. J.C. Penny was blessed. His parents trained him in the Golden Rule from infancy, and he embraced it all his life. If you have had that kind of upbringing, thank your parents. If you have not, it is still not too late to change.

Observations from a Retail Associate

You have decided to become a Retail Associate, so you now have a significant responsibility to everyone with whom you interact.

As I have mentioned before, it all starts with you. Begin by evaluating your own character.

Character – and not your circumstances – should determine your decisions.

We must take responsibility for everything we do and STOP blaming others or circumstances for anything.

Circumstances may interfere with our lives or our business, but it is how we control our attitude about these circumstances that is important.

Remember: any wrong decisions you make in your store will have a negative impact not only on your store, but also on the rest of your company.

Doing nothing is not an option. Neither is quitting.

You decided to start, so finish what you started.

Use your boss as a coach to hold you accountable.

As your coach, they will tell you what you need to hear and not what you want to hear.

What to Watch Out for When Adopting the Ethical "*Gold Standard*"

Sabotaging the Golden Rule

Carrying out what is right really does receive a great deal of consideration nowadays. How come? Simply because it is news whenever somebody practices the Golden Rule, encounters unfavorable implications for it and is happy that he did what is right.

Let us face the facts; there are numerous issues that encourage men and women to cross an ethical line. As I have worked alongside men and women and led organizations for more than 30 years, I have regrettably witnessed lots of people compromise their own standards. And I can tell you that having worked with men and women in just about every socioeconomic group in more that 170 countries around the world, in my opinion it always comes down to one of five conditions. The following are the five aspects that most frequently come up whenever an individual compromises his/her ethics:

Condition #1 – Pressure

Most of the ethical violations which keep mounting within the global marketplace and government today result from senior executives and political leaders covering up the truth. They do it to make their organizations or administrations appear more successful than they really happen to be.

A recent study by the Ethics Resource Center of Washington revealed:

Study: Ethical breaches are becoming common in government.

> *"A new report suggests that a crisis in principles and morals is looming in government and may even be underway... While government misconduct is high, it's likely to get worse... We believe that the next Enron could take place in the public sector. At present, the government lacks many of the important interventions that could reduce this risk.*
>
> *...52 percent of government employees reported witnessing misconduct by co-workers in 26 [This study is now 13 years d – is there any update, or more recent data?] ... 23 percent said they saw or experienced abusive behavior, 21 percent witnessed safety violations and 20 percent knew someone who had lied to their colleagues or was involved in a possible conflict of interest.*
>
> Most reports of misconduct involved ethical breaches, rather than legal violations, according to ERC.

> *Government employees reported 3 percent more incidents of falsifying or altering documents and 4 percent more incidents of lying to employees than their private sector counterpart did.*
>
> *… misconduct was up 12 percent from 2005, from 58 percent to 70 percent. It is highly likely that higher levels of management are unaware that misconduct is even a problem within their organization.*
>
> *… 25 percent of employees saying they worked in situations that were conducive to wrongdoing and 48 percent saying they encountered situations that invited unethical behavior.*
>
> *The public trusts that government leaders have strong ethics and make sure they're followed throughout their organizations… In setting standards, the government must look at itself."* [xxxvii]

U.S. Retailers Lead World in Data Breaches

- "U.S. retailers lead the world in security breaches, according to the 2018 Thales Data Threat Report, Retail Edition. U.S. retail data breaches more than doubled since the last Thales report, rising to 50% from 19% in the 2017 survey. The global average of retail executives reporting data breaches is 27%.
- Additionally, the number of U.S. retailers reporting a data breach at any time in the

past is up to 75% with half of those occurring in the last year. Of global retailers, 60% report at least one breach in the past. As a result, U.S. retail is now the second most breached segment analyzed by Thales, trailing the U.S. federal government only slightly and ranking ahead of healthcare and financial services.
- While 84% of the U.S. retailers polled are increasing information technology security spending, which is up from last year's 77% and exceeds global retails 67%, the Thales report said that the spending is *"in all the wrong places."* The spending is highest on security measures regarded as least effective." [xxxviii]

Within our fast-paced lifestyle, there is no doubt that just about everybody feels some type of pressure. Along with pressure comes the enticement of taking short-cuts or out-and-out lie. Publicly traded corporations have senior executives that feel pressure to improve their respective stock prices. Retail Associates feel pressure to generate more sales. Students feel pressure to obtain better grades. Not one person escapes the pressure. Therefore, the real question is: ***How are you going to deal with the pressure?***

Because you encounter daily pressure, watch out for how you could possibly be influenced to compromise your values, and ask yourself some tough questions:

As a Retail Associate, should I make hasty emotionally charged decisions?

Pressure generates anxiety, and anxiety certainly creates emotionally charged moments for some Retail Associates. Some Retail Associates have difficulty in these circumstances, and they end up making extremely poor decisions that impact themselves and/or other Retail Associates. *How can I as a Retail Associate guard against that?*

As a Retail Associate, should I compromise the simple truth?

Some Retail Associates find it nearly impossible to confess to making an error. Am I as a Reil Associate prepared to adhere to the truth regardless of whether I like it?

As a Retail Associate, should I cut corners?

It has been said that the longest distance between two points is a short-cut. While that may be true, pressure tempts us as Retail Associates to contemplate short cuts when we in any other case would not. Am I as a Retail Associate prepared to battle to carry out what is right?

As a Retail Associate, should I maintain my personal obligations?

Men and women in Retail are identical in their promises. However, it is only in their exploits that they differ. Am I as a Retail Associate likely to continue to keep my promise as well as follow through, regardless of whether it hurts or not?

As a Retail Associate, should I bend to the opinions of others?

Some Retail Associates tend to be particularly vulnerable to the opinions of others. That was true of me for the first few months as a Retail Associate. Will I as a Retail Associate carry out the things, I realize are right, regardless of whether it's popular or unpopular?

As a Retail Associate, should I make commitments I cannot preserve?

"We ought not to raise expectations which is not in our power to satisfy. It is more pleasing to see smoke brighten into flame, than flame sinking into smoke." - Samuel Jackson

How am I as a Retail Associate planning to maintain my commitments from going up in flames?

In case your objective is always to make good decisions under pressure, I would recommend that you might want reminders of exactly what is at stake. First, keep in mind that you happen to be accountable to a higher power. Second, keep in mind that you happen to be accountable to your family. I personally keep reminders of that around me all the time. On my laptop and iPad, the background picture is of my daughter, so I will never forget that people are depending on me to do right. One of my definitions of success is for those family, friends and colleagues that are closest to me love and respect me the most.

Memory joggers tend to be invaluable, however they are insufficient. Furthermore, I require systems to help keep me personally on track. For example, if I need to decide under pressure, I will spend time writing out the problem and solution, so I will not behave rashly. I take note of promises I make thus so that I can easily remember them. I additionally use software on my laptop and iPad to follow up with me on decisions and promises in order that they don't slip through the cracks. I would recommend that you do similar types of things. Do whatever you must to maintain your ethics under pressure.

Condition #2 – Pleasure

The reality is that the pleasures most of us engage in are generally short-lived and leave us unsatisfied. The things which induce us to infrequently deliver on what they promise.

Exactly what is the answer to the enticement of pleasure? The first thought should be to run quickly from enticement.

If you understand you happen to be particularly vulnerable to a certain pleasure that is going to induce you to cross an ethical line, run in the opposite direction. Whenever you observe it approaching, stop and change direction and remove yourself from that enticement. The most effective way to steer clear of enticement is to prevent it in the first place.

The second solution is to develop discipline.

"Discipline is the screw, the nail, the cement, the glue, the nut, the bolt, the rivet that holds everything tight. Discipline is the wire, the connecting rod, and the chain that coordinates. Discipline is the oil that makes machines run fast, and the oil that makes parts slide smooth as well as the oil that makes the metal bridge. They know about discipline here. The principle of discipline here is divinely simple; you lay it on thick and fast, all the time." - Private Gerald Kersh

It is interesting, but to achieve independence, you will need to contain your emotional behavior with discipline. That requires character. One of the simplest ways to develop discipline is usually to postpone pleasure.

The current generation does not accomplish that at all. We are in an "I want it now" culture. If you require further proof, look at "real-time" Debt Statistics at www.USDEBTCLOCK.org - WARNING – This page may scare you a bit if you are concerned about the debt of the United States.

- Total Personal Debt: $24.2 Trillion
- Mortage Debt: $15.6 Trillion
- Student Loan Debt: $1.76 Trillion
- Credit Card Debt: $1.2 Trillion
- National Debt: $31.4 Trillion [xxxix]

The concept of delayed versus instant gratification is undoubtedly one of the most important choices that separate rich thinking from poor thinking. And it is not a choice until you have consciously identified it as one. Since it is too often a matter of unconscious repeating of the pattern that your family or closest friends are instilling in you, it is especially important to think it through for yourself. Does no money down with fixed monthly payments really make more sense to you compared to acquiring assets that pay for what you want? Your answer should address both financial and emotional sensibility.

Retail Associates who have lost their minds to instant gratification and possessions sadly help to make themselves untrustworthy to their fellow Retail Associates. Any Retail Associate who enjoys gratification more than truth is on a path to difficulty and will unfortunately take his/her associates with them.

Condition #3 – Power

Most of the latest scandals in American business have been the result of senior executives abusing the power of their positions. These misguided people started to believe that the actual assets of the publicly traded companies they led could possibly be dealt with as their own private property. Unfortunately, for many Retail Associates, having power is like drinking saltwater. The more you drink, the thirstier you get.

Enron and WorldCom have since become popular symbols of willful corporate fraud and corruption. The scandals were also considered landmark cases in the field of business fraud and brought into question the ethical practices of many corporations throughout the United States.

Retail Associates who happen to be particularly vulnerable to power issues typically experience a cycle that follows the following pattern:

The Acquisition of Power: Power itself is neutral, like money. It is a device which can be used for good or ill. However, it can be extremely dangerous, especially for Retail Associates who progress quickly and obtain power before being ready for it.

The Misuse of Power: One of many dangers associated with power for a Retail Associate is the fact that those who find themselves trusted with it start to make its upkeep their own main objective. These Retail Associates don't seem to understand or know that the power that they have been granted, regardless of whether it's in their business, community, friends, or family, has been bestowed on them for the purpose of service. Those Retail Associates who seem to want most to maintain their power no matter what are likely to compromise typical ethical behavior to maintain it.

The Deprivation of Power: Unsurprisingly, any Retail Associate who abuses their power will lose their power. Abusive Retail Associates, like dictators, are living on borrowed time.

Power is like a grand waterway. Provided that it maintains its course, it is a beneficial masterpiece of design. However, when it floods its banks, it usually brings amazing devastation. How does a Retail Associate maintain the power of its banks? We could take a page from the 33rd President of the United States of America, Harry S. Truman. He recommended, *"If a man can accept a situation in a place of power with the thought that it's only temporary, he comes out all right. But when he thinks he is the cause of the power that can be his ruination."* Any Retail Associate who knows that they are safeguarding their power excessively ought to begin evaluating themselves for breaches of ethics. Power can be horribly seductive.

Condition #4 – Pride

You may not instantly consider pride as a prospective trap that could weaken ethics as well as work against the practice of the Golden Rule. Given the circumstances, aren't men and women admonished to take pride in their job? Don't most people encourage their own children's good behavior simply by letting them know exactly how proud they are of them? Aren't students motivated to create pride within their school?

Possessing a perception of genuine worth because of who you are is an excellent thing. Same goes with possessing confidence regarding what you do. However, possessing an embellished perception of self-worth could very well be extremely harmful.

C.S. Lewis made available a unique point of view on pride with what I believe was an excellent perception. He considered that pride contributes to each other's depravity. He stated,

"Does this seem to you exaggerated? If so, think it over. I pointed out a moment ago that the more pride one had, the more one disliked pride in others. In fact, if you want to find out how proud you are the easiest way is to ask yourself, 'How much do I dislike it when other people snub me?' The point is that each person's pride is in competition with everyone else's pride. It is because I wanted to be the big noise at the party that I am so annoyed at someone else

being the big noise... Now what you want to get clear is that Pride is essentially competitive, is competitive by its very nature, while the other vices are competitive only, so to speak, by accident.

Pride gets no pleasure out of having more of it than the next man. We say that people that people are proud of being richer, or cleverer, or better looking than others. If everyone else became equally rich, or clever, or good looking there would be nothing to be proud about. It is the comparison that makes you proud: the pleasure of being above the rest." [xl]

How can Retail Associates treat other individuals the way they want to be treated if their own engrossment is to defeat them? It is simple, they cannot. The truth is if your objective is intended to be richer, wiser, or more appealing as compared to everybody else, your concentration is completely on yourself and your own self-interests.

Over the past two decades, there appears to have been a significant decline in ethics in American society most notably in business, politics, law, and medicine. This a result of misguided pride?

Pride for a Retail Associate, like anyone else, is just not a straightforward thing to overcome.

"There is perhaps not one of our natural passions so hard to subdue as pride. Beat it down, stifle it, mortify it as much as one pleases, it is still alive. Even if I could conceive that I had completely overcome it, I should probably be proud of my humility." - Benjamin Franklin

I am in full agreement with Ben Franklin, in that it is next to impossible to fully overcome pride. We should, however, at least try to overcome it. Pride can weaken our ethics and hinder our overall performance. Pride can easily visually impair you, to your personal defects, along with other men and women's requirements, and to ethical obstacles that lay across our path.

"When dealing with people, let us remember we are not dealing with creatures of logic. We are dealing with creatures of emotion, creatures bustling with prejudices and motivated by pride and vanity." - Dale Carnegie

Condition #5 – Priorities

Over the past several years, substantial research has been undertaken into exactly what tends to make businesses extremely prosperous.

"Our research points to one essential element in any successful company. Those that are the best have built a set of core values and lived by them." - Jim Collins

This is also true for the men and women in the Retail Sector. Any time a man or a woman does not understand what his or her priorities need to be he or she can easily discover themselves struggling, simply because he or she is most likely to make extremely poor decisions.

"Things that matter most must never be at the mercy of things that matter least." - Goethe

As a Retail Associate, exactly what are your priorities? Precisely what are you currently carrying out now that will still be essential in 50 or 100 years. The material things in life, such as the house you live in, the car you drive, the vacation you took, and the bonus you made will not mean much. As a Retail Associate, precisely what genuinely matters? If you have not determined your values, I highly encourage you to do so. Then work tirelessly to help keep the insignificant from becoming significant, and the significant from becoming insignificant.

Maintaining the Brilliance on the "*Gold Standard*"

It is possible you have realized that greed did not make the list of aspects that could "*discolor*" the Golden Rule. That could possibly come as a shock, particularly considering that the mainstream media have spoken a great deal about it lately with all the current corporate and business scandals. In the Retail Sector, I am of the belief that, often, it's not necessarily the cash itself that draws men and women across the line ethically. I believe that it's exactly what they could possibly get with it. These Retail Associates want the power that cash brings, regardless of whether it's power over other associates or over circumstances. These Retail Associates just want the pleasure that can be purchased with cash. Or these Retail Associates take pride in the actual status of possessions that the cash buys.

If you discover a man or woman in the Retail Sector who will give up their integrity for money, I genuinely believe you will discover that it is motivated by one of the five conditions previously mentioned.

In the Retail Sector, like everywhere else, men and women are vulnerable to some type of enticement to give up their values. However, the encouraging news is that there is a significantly greater fulfillment which comes from not crossing the line. Occasionally you will need to wait for it. Nevertheless, it will invariably arrive.

Observations from a Retail Associate

Let the *"Golden Rule"* be your navigation system. Do not under any circumstances undermine what could be the most valuable part of your life and business.

I have personally witnessed the following:

Upper management putting pressure on associates that are part of their team to do something that is not in their best interest but is in the best interest of upper management.

Over promising on the opportunity and never delivering on the promises.

Management using their position to strong arm their staff.

Management making bad and unethical decisions, and then continues the unethical practice so that no one loses face.

Management inserts their personal priorities into their associate's lives, without considering the associate's position.

Etc...

STOP! Everything you do needs to be in the best interest of the customer and thus the business.

End of story.

Carpe Diem and the Ethical "*Gold Standard*"

I am of the viewpoint that most men and women in the Retail Sector are searching for a "*golden opportunity.*"

Just out of curiosity, I searched Google for "*golden opportunity*" (a chance to do something that is likely to be successful and rewarding) and 0.66 seconds it returned 504,000,000 results.

Most of the Retail Associates believe that their best opportunity comes from the company they chose to join. However, the simple truth I that the best opportunity a Retail Associate has is the same as anyone else; it is to transform who you are. It is like giving a position on a Stanley Cup winning team to a yoga instructor who has not trained for their event. The good news is that the yoga instructor has been given a shot at winning. The not so good news is that the yoga instructor is not prepared for it.

How One Step Leads to the Next Step

It seems apparent that it was a similar kind of challenge for quite a few of the CEOs who ended their careers with a big bang and demolished their businesses during the past decade. These kinds of "*special*" men and women had not carried out the ethical preparation internally prior to attaining power. It ended up being their poor character that persuaded these "*people of influence*" to make extremely bad decisions, and with just about every bad decision, these men and women got themselves and their companies into much deeper difficulties. Character challenges are like a snowball rolling down a hill, once it starts, it gets bigger and bigger until finally it reaches the bottom of the hill totally out of control and takes out your neighbor.

It seems that good and evil equally increase in a similar fashion to the way money increases using the power of compound interest. That is the reason why the small choices we me every single day possess such unlimited significance. The tiniest, good action performed now is the catalyst for which there is a chance you can win or wins you have never dreamed of before. And a lack of action today is something that can come back in the future and bite you in the ass. (Personally, I can attest to this one.)

As a Retail Associate, prior to looking to your company as the "*golden opportunity*," start pursuing the growth and development of powerful character. This will certainly position you extremely well to manage any ethical challenge that could possibly lie in the future and to take full advantage of your possibilities as soon as your time arrives. Here is how I suggest you proceed:

As a Retail Associate, Make Every Single Action You Take Your Responsibility

This is a concept that is lost on some Retail Associates. If you happen to be involved, no matter what it is, you are responsible for your actions! Obligation is in proportion to the opportunity available to you and me. Do you understand why? Due to the fact any man or woman of responsibility can easily trust in or herself to select the right thing above the easy thing.

The definition of *"frustration"* for some Retail Associates is *"having no one to blame but yourself."* rarely do men and women of the Retail Sector who take part in the *"blame game"* get hold of very many *"golden opportunities."* And in some cases, the very few opportunities these men and women do get a hold of fall right through their fingertips. Whenever that takes place, undoubtedly, you will hear that the reason is not their fault.

There is simply no excuse for falling into any of these categories:

The "*Life's Circumstances*" Attribution – Retail Associates who seem to pin the circumstances on life's conditions,

The "*Woe is Me*" Attribution – Retail Associates who seem to pin the consequences on previous personal challenges and injuries, and

The *"Manure Spreader"* Attribution – Retail Associates who seem to pin the consequence on various other retail associates for working against them.

If it happens to be your wish to be trusted by other Retail Associates and you also desire to be successful, you will first need to assume responsibility regarding your actions. Responsibility here means the actual preparation regarding opportunity, as well as the cost of success.

As a Retail Associate, Your Personal Discipline Must Be Developed

Not long ago I read the results of a recent study of more than 400 business executives that reveals that many people who cheat at golf also cheat in business. *"Those who move the ball for a better lie or conveniently forget to count a couple of strokes are also likely to fake reports, juggle accounts, and lie about their business actions. Asked if they cheated at golf, 55% admitted they did... The challenge now facing America's business executives, as I see it, is not to explain themselves better, but to demonstrate that they take t public's concerns and criticisms seriously. It's time for Americans to elect Arnold Palmer or Jack Nicklaus President – someone who understands not only the rules of the game but the importance of playing by them whether he or she is being watched or not. Professional golfers are the only professionals I know who call penalties on themselves for violating the rules of the game. Frankly, I would like to see that kind of honesty in our nation's leaders and in its business leaders, as well. We need leaders who not only hit the ball straight, but who think straight and talk straight, too."* [xli]

Polls, as any pollster knows, sometimes reveals what men and women think, not necessarily the way they act. Do you know why regardless of whether men and women notice a parallel between games and life, these men and women nonetheless make the decision to take shortcuts? The answer lies in their lack of discipline. Men and women who neglect to develop personal discipline in many cases are inclined to cheat just to keep up with society. Expertise without having discipline is like a baby trying to walk for the very first time. At first, there is abundance of movement, however, you cannot say for sure if it's destined to be forward, backwards, or back onto their nicely padded bums.

As a Retail Associate, precisely what we choose to do at any given time will in all probability be determined by what we are made of; and just what we are made of is the result of previous years of self-discipline.

Retail Associates who would like to enhance their character in addition to their likelihood of success need to discipline themselves when it comes to:

Chronology: You cannot regulate how much time you are allotted, nevertheless you can manage the way you utilize it.

Drive: It is recommended to always try to make use of your strengths.

Objectives: You cannot accomplish everything, which means you need to discipline yourself to carry out the essential things.

Temperament: Unless you master your emotions, they will master you.

Highly effective Retail Associates, who work well with others, thrive on challenges and business opportunities, and don't find discipline to be detrimental or even prohibitive. Over the past 3 years I have had the pleasure of meeting hundreds of Retail Associates, and I can tell you one thing, the ones that are striving to be at the top of their game love the daily grind and discipline.

As a Retail Associate, You Need to Realize Your Weaknesses

For almost two and a half decades I had the opportunity to listen to and learn from Dexter and Birdie Yager of Amway fame. Several times a year, in locations across the United States and overseas I would stand stage-side and listen to both Dexter and Birdie speak. Now it's important to understand that they would not come on stage until about 1:00 to 2:00 a.m. and speak for 3+

hours. And this is during a weekend event that began at 9:00 a.m. and did not usually end until the wee hours of the morning on Friday and Saturday. This talk that Dexter and Birdie offered was not traditional-style training; it was training about life. A lot of the topics were controversial, and I did not necessarily agree with all that was said, but I loved the dedication of the craft, as well as how they both knew their weaknesses and did something about them.

As a Retail Associate, to know about your weaknesses in advance allows you to prepare yourself and make the necessary changes inside. Men and women who recognize their own weaknesses are hardly ever taken by surprise, neither do they permit other individuals to take advantage of their weaknesses. In distinction, men and women who fool themselves or who pretend that they are strong where they're not just set themselves up to fail.

As a Retail Associate, Your Priorities Need to Line Up Together with Your Values

Integrity can easily be called making your values and actions fall into line. When a Retail Associate states they believe one thing and then they intentionally take an opposing action, it's apparent that exactly what they lack is integrity. However, what about a Retail Associate who does not comprehend that his or her steps oppose his or her values? Even though it's not necessarily purposeful, that man or woman still possesses an integrity problem.

So, how does a Retail Associate ensure that their values and priorities align?

It is important to understand what integrity really is. The simplest definition of integrity is the state of being whole, entire, or undiminished. Thus, if you happen to be declaring one thing but doing another, you are divided. As a result, you have an integrity problem.

"A house divided against itself cannot stand." - Abraham Lincoln

For the Retail Associate, the perfect solution is straightforward, however certainly not simple. What is it?

- Define your values.
- Align your priorities.

As a Retail Associate, Acknowledge Wrongdoing Swiftly and Request Forgiveness

A particularly important factor which has regrettably characterized most of the recent much-discussed corporate failures is some type of concealment. Senior level executives at Enron, Tyco, and WorldCom etc., all attempted to conceal virtually every wrongdoing. That attitude is not pervasive simply in business. Men and women of poor character tend to be a lot quicker to conceal compared to admitting wrongdoing.

Let us Compare the Example Above with Jack Welch, Chairman and C.E.O 1981-2001, General Electric

Through the 1980's, Welch sought to streamline GE. In 1981 he made a speech in New York City called *"Growing fast in a slow-growth economy."* Welch worked to eradicate perceived inefficiency by trimming inventories and dismantling the bureaucracy that had almost led him to leave GE in the past. He closed factories, reduced payrolls, and cut lackluster old-line units. Welch's public philosophy was that a company should be either No. 1 or No. 2 in an industry, or else leave it completely. Welch's strategy was later adopted by other CEOs across corporate America.

Each year, Welch would fire the bottom 10% of his managers. He earned a reputation for brutal candor in his meetings with executives. He rewarded those in the top 20% with bonuses and stock options. He also expanded the broadness of the stock options program at GE from just top executives to nearly one-third of all employees. Welch is also known for destroying the nine-layer management hierarchy and bringing a sense of informality to the company.

During the 1980's he was dubbed *"Neutron Jack"* (in reference to the neutron bomb) for eliminating employees while leaving buildings intact. In *Jack: Straight from the Gut*, Welch states that GE had 411,000 employees (about half the population of Montana) at the end of 1980, and 299,000 at the end of 1985. Of the 112,000 who left the payroll, 37,000 were in businesses that GE sold, and 81,000 were reduced in continuing businesses. In return, GE increased its market capital tremendously. Welch reduced basic research and closed or sold off businesses that were under-performing.

In 1986, GE acquired RCA. RCA's corporate headquarters were in Rockefeller Center; Welch subsequently took up an office in the then GE Building at 30 Rockefeller Plaza. The RCA acquisition resulted in GE selling off RCA properties to other companies and keeping NBC as part of the GE portfolio of businesses. During the 1990s, Welch shifted GE business from manufacturing to financial services through numerous acquisitions.

Welch adopted Motorola's Six Sigma quality program in late 1995. In 1980, the year before Welch became Chief Executive Officer, GE recorded revenues of roughly $26.8 billion (about $82 per person in the US). By 1999 he was named "Manager of the Century" by Fortune magazine. In 2000, the year before he left, the revenues increased to $130 billion (about $400 per person in the US). The company had gone from a market value of $14 billion (about $43 per person in the US) to one of more than $410 billion (about $1,300 per person in the US) at the end of 2004, making it the most valuable company in the world.

Prior to his retirement, there was a lengthy and well-publicized succession planning saga among James McNerney, Robert Nardelli, and Jeffrey Immelt, with Immelt eventually selected to succeed Welch as Chairman and Chief Executive Officer. Nardelli became the Chief Executive Officer of Home Depot until his resignation in early 2007, and until recently, was the Chief Executive Officer of Chrysler, while McNerney became Chief Executive Officer of 3M until he left that post to serve in the same capacity at Boeing.

Welch's severance package was valued at $417 million according to Forbes magazine.

So, what is the comparison between my example above and that of Jack Welch's tenure as Chairman and Chief Executive Officer at General Electric?

Welch carried out the ethical preparation internally prior to attaining power. His character and decision-making capabilities added so much value back to GE that he was worth every dime he was paid, and his percentage of value added was off the charts.

As a Retail Associate, Your Finances Require Extra Care

One of the better approaches to accumulate awareness of the character of another Retail Associate is to watch exactly how they manage their money. To gain an even better insight into the topic of managing money, ask the following questions.

- Are Retail Associates generous with other people's money but restricted to making use of their own?
- Do these Retail Associates demand that each financial transaction naturally benefits them?
- Do these Retail Associates take shortcuts to realize even more wealth?
- Precisely what place does money rank in the lives of Retail Associates?

Cash does not transform men and women; it simply reveals what is truly inside them. If a man or woman is normally self-centered or conceited or money grubbing, the cash brings that out for all to see.

Men and women can frequently be tripped up whenever they make amassing greater wealth a greater priority than it ought to be.

I pointed out in a previous chapter that money is certainly nothing more than a tool. However, it is important to point out that it is a very razor-sharp tool; one which if dealt with badly can-do amazing damage. That is the reason why we as Retail Associates need to take special care of our finances. If we as Retail Associates manage the appropriate attitude towards money, then it will invariably be a beneficial, valuable tool and not a detrimental one.

If you are concerned about keeping money from becoming the master, try doing the following:

As a Retail Associate, Generate Your Own Personal Income – Men and women who generate what they have gotten have a much greater regard for the property of other men and women. And with this type of mindset as a Retail Associate you will attempt to receive more bangs for your buck if you must earn it yourself.

As a Retail Associate, Always Be Meticulously Trustworthy – Bend over backwards to ensure your complete financial transactions are above board, not merely regarding others, but in addition for yourself.

As a Retail Associate, Become Generous – You often hear that we earn a living by what we generate; however, we make a life by what we donate or tithe. Donating or tithing not only assists other individuals as well as liberates all of us; additionally, it puts money into the proper perspective much better than anything else you or I can do.

As a Retail Associate, Make Use of Credit Sensibly and Moderately – Ok, before you jump all over me and say, *"Kevin, how do I do that when just about everything requires a credit card, especially purchases online?"* Simple, let us first look back at our goal. Use credit sensibly and moderately. First, only use your credit card when you need to. Secondly, be sensible and pay off the balance every 30 days (or prior to your next statement) so that you minimize your accumulation of interest.

As a Retail Associate, learning how to have the appropriate attitude with regards to money, as well as how to manage it appropriately (instead of being handled by it) sets the groundwork for several additional character triumphs in a Retail Associates life.

As a Retail Associate, Place Your Family in Advance of Your Business

The variety of job titles and political positions he has attained is remarkable: U.S. Congressman, Ambassador to the United Nations, Chief Liaison Officer in China, Head of the CIA, Vice President of the United States, and finally, President of the United States. However, when his life in public office concluded, George H.W. Bush declared that he continued to possess the three most significant titles ever held: husband, father, and grandfather.

Without a doubt, that is an awesome perspective on family.

As a Retail Associate, Place High Value on Men and Women

Whenever the majority of Retail Associates take into consideration the development of character, these men and women concentrate on whatever they need to turn out to be, which is excellent, considering that this is much of the course of action required.

However, in order to make yourself prepared to take hold of the *"golden opportunities,"* you need to do one more thing. As a Retail Associate you need to value other men and women sufficiently to provide them with a portion of yourself, which is your trust. That, given the circumstances, is without a doubt the real heart and soul of the Golden Rule.

Years ago, I heard this story told from a stage at a seminar, about how a naval commander by the name of Mike Abrashoff lived the Golden Rule both onboard and on land.

I was always taught that when telling a story from stage, ensure that you tie a point that you are trying to make to that story.

Mike Abrashoff graduated from the U.S. Naval Academy in Annapolis, attained the rank of captain after sixteen years, became military assistant to Dr. William J. Perry when he was Secretary of Defense and then his first command, the USS Benfold where the story of the Golden Rule truly begins.

For the first sixteen years of Mike's career, he went for the gold braid (promotions). He had plenty of success, however for the Navy, it was not an uncommon success. The very last two years Mike decided to go for the Golden Rule. Mike took command of the USS Benfold and of his life. Prior to these two years, Mike had been operating in accordance with what he believed were the navy's objectives. However, while working for Secretary of Defense Perry, he observed a disengagement from that kind of thought process. When Mike observed his predecessor departing the ship, he thought about what his departure would turn out to be like.

Mike always explained the Navy as being remarkably similar to a tree packed with monkeys. If you happen to be at the top of the tree (senior level officer and above), all you ever observe whenever you look down is a bunch of smiling faces looking right back at you. However, if you happen to be a monkey at the bottom of the tree and you look up, your view is best described as *"different."*

Mike decided to put himself in the shoes of his sailors. Mike individually and independently interviewed each and every sailor on his ship to determine exactly what each of these sailors valued, after which Mike implemented modifications in response to what the sailors valued, for example sending the ships cooks to culinary school to become chefs, as well as providing college and University courses on-board his ship. Mike decided to ask his officers to treat the newly arriving sailors as they quite simply would want their own children treated (how cool is that). And Mike enabled each and every sailor on board, no matter what rank they held, to generate decisions and make an effort to turn their ship into the best in the Navy, by simply having faith in them and inspiring them with words: *"It's your ship."*

Mike quickly noticed that as soon as he started to strive for the Golden Rule, good began to happen on the ship. The moment that Mike started to put men and women instead of a promotion first, the results were positive and exponential. That is exactly what I would refer to as taking advantage of a *"golden opportunity."*

Observations from a Retail Associate

If you would like to build a strong foundation in your Retail organization, here is how I suggest you proceed:

Take Responsibility for Your Actions – Everything you do or don't do is your responsibility. The faster you adopt this mind-set the faster your organization will grow.

Develop Personal Discipline – You must be able to lead by example. How many Retail Associates would you like in your company with the same personal discipline that you possess today?

Know Your Weaknesses – Know your weaknesses but do not dwell on them. Build your company to backfill the weaknesses.

Align Your Priorities with Your Values – It all starts with your values. From there your priorities need to be set.

Admit Wrongdoing Quickly and Ask Forgiveness – It is simple. However, it may not be easy. Suck it up and admit your wrongdoing and move on.

Take Extra care with Finances – Once again, lead by example.

Put Your Family Ahead of Your Work – This is critical. Why else are you working unless it is for your family? Spend quality time with your family and ensure that they are behind you in your endeavor. Place High Value on People.

The Following Steps Will Help You Implement the Ethical "Gold Standard"

The Genuine Gold Standard

Today, it is hard not to be selfish, at least a little bit. It is an element of human nature. However, if you are doing so an excessive amount, people in your circle of influence could possibly get sick and tired of you. Here is how to stop being selfish:

- Try to develop empathy for other people and living creatures. Allow yourself to imagine how they feel, what hurts them or makes them happy. Open your heart.
- Look for ways to help; anticipate the needs and feelings of others.
- Listen. There is an enormous difference between hearing something and letting something go in one ear and out the other and listening to what people have to say.
- Do not interrupt people. Let them finish their sentence, your points can always wait. If it's urgent (like if you must leave) say *"excuse me."*
- Put the needs of other people before your own. Pay attention to the people in your life to find out what those needs are.

- Think about the other person's personality. When choosing gifts or cards, buy something that reflects the personality of the other person. Do not just buy something because it is convenient.
- Remember birthdays.
- Stay connected with your friends and relatives.
- Volunteer.
- Be honest and loyal.
- Consider the advice people in your life give you. Take it if it makes sense.
- If you must ask someone for a favor, offer to do something for him or her in return.
- Compliment other people. Do not just go on about how great you are.
- Make sure to be considerate and include everyone you know and like when inviting people to parties and events. No one likes to be left out.
- Do not butt in front of people in line. Also, if you see someone in a walker or a wheelchair, slow down or help them instead of just cutting in front of them.
- Be on time. If possible, call if you know you are going to be late.

- Give your time or kindness to others that need it. Random acts of kindness also make you feel satisfied.

Introducing the Gold Standard 3.0 Life

I am of the belief that you will find there's actual true wealth that happens to be more significant than money, and it originates from the method in which you connect with other men and women. Men and women who apply the Golden Rule treat other individuals with dignity as well as respect and can be fulfilled knowing that they happen to be living an ethical life.

However, I am here to tell you that it's possible to take the Golden Rule to a level above all others, and I call it the *"Gold Standard 3.0!"*

Gold Standard 3.0 is when you establish a *"Midas Touch"* with men and women by removing the focus off yourself and precisely what you will gain, and as an alternative, devote 100% of your time to adding value to others.

Giving genuinely is the pinnacle of living. Without question, it helps make our global community a much better place to live. And coincidently it tends to make for a much better company. As Retail Associates, we would certainly possess a much better industry when we realize that the highest dividends are paid when we invest in the development of global *"human resources."* If you would like to truly invest in men and women, then try to live out the following practices:

As a Retail Associate, Treat Men and Women Much Better Than These Men and Women Happen to Treat You

We all know that it's an easy task to love the men and women who happen to love us. And deep down within all of us we know that displaying kindness to men and women who happen to treat us well is a bit more than simple common courtesy. However exactly how should we as Retail Associates react to bad treatment by other men and women? Should we return discourtesy with discourtesy? Should we meet encroachment with encroachment? It does not require a sociologist to tell us that it does not take much for unkindness to escalate into greater discord. Have a look at a few of these obviously insignificant squabbles that progressed into a full-blown war:

- A disagreement involving the cities of Modena and Bologna, in northern Italy, over a water well bucket about 900 years ago began a war that devastated Europe.
- A Chinese Emperor on one occasion went to war over the smashing of a teapot.
- Sweden and Poland flew at each other's throats in 1654 because the King of Sweden learned that his name in an

official dispatch was followed by only two "*et cetera's,*" while the King of Poland had three.
- The spilling of a glass of water on the Marque de Torey led to a war between France and England.
- By throwing a pebble at the Duc de Guise, a small boy caused the massacre of Vassy and the Thirty Years' War.

It requires a Retail Associate of formidable character to treat other individuals better than they treat you. If all Retail Associates practiced the Golden Rule, our global community would be a much better place to be. However, take into consideration what type of global community it would be like if every Retail Associate endeavored to treat other Retail Associates much better than they are treated themselves (perhaps adopt that mindset at home).

WELCOME TO THE GOLD STANDARD 3.0!

As a Retail Associate, Walk the Second Mile

What is the second mile and where did that expression come from?

In the 3rd century B.C., and for 500 years after, the Roman Empire allowed a Roman Officer to force anyone to carry a load one mile. It was the officer's right, and a citizen who declined did so at his own peril. This first mile was a requirement, however, any length beyond that was a show of respect to the Roman officer. Thus, the second mile was born, and the expression *"Walk the Second Mile"* began.

So, what do I mean when I suggest walking the second mile in the Retail Sector? I am suggesting that you strive to do more than is required. Try and look at the extra mile as being an opportunity to make a positive impact on the lives of other Retail Associates, and to add value to the men and women in your life.

A Retail Associate that possesses an *"extra-mile"* attitude is a man or woman who:

- Cares more about others than others think is wise.
- Risk more for others than others think is safe.

- Dreams more than others think are practical.
- Expects more than others think is possible.
- Works more than others think is necessary.

"There's no traffic jam on the extra mile." - Zig Ziglar

If you as a Retail Associate consistently carry out a lot more than what is anticipated, not only are you going to rise above the masses, but you will also assist other individuals to rise along with you.

Have you at any time sat back and thought that it appeared like lots of people in this world are not carrying out their own fair share of work?

The following is a survey that consists of 100 percent irrefutable statistics and proves without a shadow of a doubt that there are not nearly as many people working as you may have thought, and you have absolutely every reason to be tired.

- In the United States of America, the population is a bit over 315 million. [xlii]
    - In the United States, there is a birth every 8 seconds, and death every 11 seconds.
    - 106 million people are over the age of 64 and retired. That leaves 209 million people to do all the work.

- People under 20 years of age total 119 million, so that leaves 90 million to do all the work.
- There are 34 million who are employed by the government, which leaves 56 million to do the work.
- 18 million are in the armed forces, which leaves 38 million to do all the work.
- Deduct 25 million, the number in state and city offices. That leaves 13 million to do the work.
- There are 9 million in hospitals, mental institutions, and various asylums, so that leaves 4 million to do the work.
- Now it may interest you to know that there are approximately 3,999,998 people (about twice the population of New Mexico) in jails and prisons, so that just leaves 2 people to carry the load! ☐

That is, you and me, and I am about to get ready for a break!

As a Retail Associate, Assist Men and Women Who Cannot Help You Back

You and I have not lived today effectively unless we have performed something for someone unable to repay us.

If as a Retail Associate you desire to live a Gold Standard 3.0 life, then do something for someone who can never repay you and do it consistently.

JAMAICAN NATIONAL BOBSLED TEAM

The Jamaican national bobsled team represented Jamaica in International bobsledding competitions, and first gained fame during their debut in the 1988 Winter Olympic Games in Calgary, Alberta, Canada, where they were underdogs, representing a tropical nation in a winter sport. The team returned to the Winter Olympics again in 1992, 1994, and subsequent competitions. The team failed to qualify for the 2006 and 2010 Winter Olympics.

The team (consisting of Devon Harris, Dudley Stokes, Michael White, and Nelson Stokes) quickly became a fan favorite largely because of their status position as the ultimate *"underdog"* story of the games. Not only was there the novelty of having a tropical country compete in a cold-weather sport, but they had very little practice going down a bobsled track before, and they borrowed spare sleds from other countries to compete. In a show of worldly brotherhood, other bobsledders were quick to give them guidance and support. They did not officially finish after losing control of the sled and crashing during one of their four runs. However, they showed significant improvement throughout the games and impressed observers with some fast starts.

This team was the inspiration for a major motion picture, Cool Runnings featuring John Candy as the team's coach. [xliii]

If you want to help people, then embrace the motto of nineteenth century evangelist D.L. Moody, who advised:

Do all you can

To all the people you can

In all the ways you can

For as long as you can.

And whenever you can do that for people who cannot do anything for you in return, then you are really developing your Gold Standard 3.0, because you are adding value to the lives of others.

Need inspiration regarding helping people? Look here:

- Donate your time to a local charity
- Do what you do best for someone for free
- Foster a homeless animal
- Volunteer at your local school
- Volunteer for a local non-profit whose work is one of your passions
- Take your pet to an assisted living center to visit
- Inspire others
- Pick a cause and lobby for it
- Bake a cake for a neighbor
- Pay for someone else's toll

- Donate money and time
- Organize your co-workers to take on a cause
- Send an email about how people can make a difference
- Give up one Saturday to do something to help
- Make a difference in your community
- Fundraising for a needy family
- Scrapbook for a "*Make-A-Wish*" child
- Donate meals for a needy family
- Learn about a charity in need and inform others
- Become a Big Brother or Sister
- Invite a less fortunate child to participate in activities with your family
- Collect toys for children in foster care
- Teach someone to read
- See a need? Fill it

As a Retail Associate, Carry Out Things That Are Right When It is Natural to Do the Wrong Things

My favorite example of someone carrying out a task when it would have been natural to do the wrong thing is the story of Cynthia Cooper and her role as whistle-blower, resulting in the downfall of WorldCom.

So, who is Cynthia Cooper you ask? Well, she is not a politician and has never run for public office. And yet without her efforts, the Sarbanes-Oxley Act – the most sweeping investor-protection legislation passed by Congress since the Great Depression – might never have been enacted.

In early 2002, following the collapse of Enron, angry lawmakers held hearings, threatened auditors, and warned CEOs that sleight-of-hand accounting tricks would not be tolerated. The Justice Department even indicted one auditing firm, Arthur Anderson, essentially putting it out of business.

But by June of 2002, the sound and fury surrounding Enron's collapse had subsided. Congress planned to pass some form of legislation, but the passions that swayed lawmakers in the winter of 2002 had eased. Business as usual was coming back into fashion.

Then WorldCom dropped a bombshell: It disclosed a $3.8 billion (about $12 per person in the US) accounting fraud of its own, sowing panic among investors. The company filed for bankruptcy protection, wiping out its shareholders, and the public demanded immediate action. Congress complied, passing the law known as the Sarbanes-Oxley act.

But the only reason WorldCom's board of directors discovered the accounting fraud was through the efforts of the company's internal auditor, Cynthia Cooper, and her dedicated subordinates.

Cynthia Cooper's adventures at WorldCom come to life in her personal account. The Mississippi native describes how, early in 2002, at the request of a colleague, she began investigating some unusual accounting entries over at WorldCom's wireless division. Little did she know at the time, but Cooper had picked up a thread that would eventually lead to WorldCom's accounting manipulations.

She approached a partner at WorldCom's auditing firm, Arthur Anderson, to discuss the matter further. The Anderson partner assured her that any aggressive accounting entries in wireless are balanced out on a corporation wide basis.

The next day, Cooper left work early to squeeze in an appointment at the hairdresser. With an 8-month-old daughter at home, it's a rare opportunity for some quiet time. But while she is in the middle of the bleaching process, shrouded in tin foil, with hairdryers blaring all around, she gets a call saying that Scott Sullivan, WorldCom's boy-wonder chief financial officer, wants to speak to her immediately.

She phones into the office, and Sullivan chides her for snooping around the wireless accounting entries. He tells her not to discuss the matter with Anderson auditors, but to channel all her queries through his own deputy, David Myers.

It is like a scene from a blockbuster thriller. Cooper has no idea that Sullivan is hiding a massive fraud that will result in the biggest bankruptcy in U.S. history, sending him and his boss to jail, but her gut instinct tells her that something is wrong.

"No one wants to believe their boss is perpetrating a fraud, you want to believe there is a valid explanation." - Cynthia Cooper

After several months, Cooper's team figures out that Sullivan's department has made $3.8 billion in questionable accounting entries that had the effect of inflating WorldCom's earnings.

Sullivan, the CFO, ultimately pleaded guilty to several crimes and testified on behalf of the government against WorldCom CEO Bernie Ebbers. Ebbers was convicted and sentenced to 25 years in prison. Sullivan, because of his cooperation, got five years. [xliv]

As a Retail Associate, Keep Your Promises Even If It Hurst Like Hell

Have you ever made a promise to a child and then were not able to keep that promise? That is among the worst things you could ever do to your child.

In late 2009 I began to feel significant pain if I happened to sit too long (no problem, at the time I sat at the computer every day for 10 to 12 hours). A few months later, in January 2010, I met with my General Physician and began a long and painful investigation into this pain's source.

By April of 2010 after seeing a Urologist and General Surgeon, we started the imaging process. However, by May 2010 without any answers, the pain became unbearable, and with two emergency visits in as many weekends, I was finally admitted to hospital.

I will spare you the unpleasant details (they are quite spectacular and can completely shut down a conversation), and only say that in 2010 I had one surgery and in 2011 I had two and 2012 another two surgeries and 2013 one surgery. During both 2010, 2011, 2011, 2011, 2011,2012 and 2013 I spent most of my time in bed and on a significant dose of painkillers, unable to work.

As 2012 neared its end and the pain lessened slightly, I began to move around a bit more and attempted to work but found it difficult with the pain limit and pain killer dosage. In December, I began to feel what I can best describe as a pain within a pain. In February 2013 on a routine visit to my surgeon, we discovered that the problem had returned and that I would require additional surgery (6 surgeries in 3 years for the same problem).

During this time, I had fully removed myself from making commitments to social functions or family outings. My modus operandi was that I would have to wait to see how I was feeling at the time of departure. I am sure you can guess that 98% of the time, I stayed home in bed.

In March 2013, I made a stupid mistake and promised my daughter (7 years old) that I would attend her gymnastics competition. Big mistake!

I was not able to attend; however, I was able to put her to bed that evening. As I lay with her, her head on my shoulder, I listened to her tell me all about her competition. I could hear her try to hold back the sobs, but the tears seemed to burn as they dampened my shirt.

That was my "literal" lesson on Keeping Your Promise Even If It Hurts Like Hell.

THE GOLD STANDARD

As a Retail Associate, where are you presently centering your attention? Are you attempting to build a **Gold Standard 3.0** life? What opportunities are you presently going after? If you were able to seize them, just what rewards are they going to bring? Would they bring wealth? How about a promotion? Would they bring recognition? Will your walls be filled with awards? Let us put them in perspective. Take this quiz:

- Name the five wealthiest people in the world.
- Name the last five Heisman Trophy winners.
- Name the last five winners of the Miss America contest.
- Name ten Retail Associates that have won the Nobel Prize.
- Name the last half-dozen Academy Award winners for best actor and actress.
- Name the last decade's World Series winners.

So, just how well did you do? Exactly how many names did you know? 75%? 50%? 25%? These men and women and their teams, the absolute best in the world at what they do, have accomplished a considerable amount. These men and women have demonstrated that they possess the special touch in their specialization, and as a result they have accomplished an amazing amount of personal recognition. However, exactly what type of influence do they have? More specifically, how much influence have they had on you? (Obviously not much if you cannot even remember most of their names).

Now, I want you to take another quiz:

- Name three teachers who inspired you to achieve in school.
- Name three friends who helped you through a challenging time.
- Name five Retail Associates who taught you something worthwhile.
- Name three Retail Associates who made you feel appreciated and special.
- Name five Retail Associates with whom you enjoy spending time.
- Name a dozen heroes whose stories have inspired you.

You may very well not have scored 100% on the second quiz either, however, I am confident that your score ended up being much better than on the very first one. Why am I confident? Simply because these would have been the men and women who had the golden touch in your own life. Adding value to you appeared to be extremely important to them. These men and women focused on other individuals, not merely on getting ahead themselves. If you wish to do something which is likely to make an impact over and above your own life, then treat men and women much better than they treat you, walk the extra mile, help people who cannot help you, do right when it's natural to do wrong, and keep your promises even when it hurts.

Observations from a Retail Associate

It starts today with a decision. Remember, from this point forward, you are responsible for your actions and inactions.

Making Sure It is Real – Remember, everything you decide in your business has either a positive or negative impact on more than just you. In Retail, there is no room for selfish thinking.

How Not to Be Fooled – Start looking for ways to give to others. This will keep you focused on other Retail Associates and not yourself.

As a Retail Associate, You Need to Treat Men and Women Much Better Than These People Happen to Treat You – This may sound odd but giving back more than you would expect will come back to you exponentially.

As a Retail Associate, Be Prepared to Walk the Second Mile – If you are not willing to walk the extra mile, do not expect others to do it. This is about your fellow Retail Associates. Do not expect them to do what you do. Remember: they will do about 50% of what you do right and 100% of what you do wrong. As a Retail Associate, be prepared to help people who can't help you.

Helping people is not about getting something back in return. It is about doing the right thing. Start looking for ways to help others that do not benefit you. You will be surprised how it positively affects your business and your life.

As a Retail Associate, Do What's Right When It is Natural to Do the Wrong Things – If it is natural to do the wrong thing, watch out, it will come back to bite you! And guess what, you will not even know where it came from!

Do the right thing 100% of the time. Think of it this way: what percentage of faithful would you like your spouse to be in your relationship?

As a Retail Associate, Always Keep Your Promises Even If It Hurts Like Hell – Sometimes we make a promise that, if kept, will have a negative fiscal impact. Keep it anyway. Not only is it the right thing to do, but you will be amazed at the goodwill it will produce. If you are trying to build a strong business, stop thinking about the small picture and adopt big picture thinking!

Conclusion: Pursue the Ethical Gold Standard Life

In wrapping up this book, I want to conclude by simply asking you, as a Retail Associate, two final questions.

1. **As a Retail Associate, exactly what would you like to accomplish?**
    a. Precisely what goals have you established for you and your family?
    b. Exactly where do you wish your career to take you?
    c. Just what impact on your own community or the global community do you desire to make?
    d. It is extremely helpful to take into consideration these kinds of factors mainly because it really helps establish the path for your life.
2. **As a Retail Associate, exactly how do you plan to accomplish it?**

That is essential mainly because it establishes the mood pertaining to exactly how you will live your life, as well as influences precisely how you are going to turn out.

There are a couple of fundamental paths to achieve a Retail Associate can choose. First, you may opt to go for the gold. Second, you can pursue a **Gold Standard 3.0** life that is supercharged by the Golden Rule.

In our world, there have been countless men and women out there who have pursued the gold and who appear to have accomplished pretty much all life has to offer. However, appearances can often be misleading.

1923 EDGEATER BEACH HOTEL, CHICAGO – THE NINE FINANCIERS, A PARABLE ABOUT POWER

The legend has it that in 1923, a meeting of America's most powerful men took place at the Edgewater Beach Hotel in Chicago. Attending the meeting were the following nine financiers and power brokers:

- The president of America's largest steel company,
- The president of America's largest utility company,
- The president of America's largest gas company,
- The president of the New York Stock Exchange,
- The president of the Bank of International Settlements,

- The nation's greatest wheat speculator,
- The nation's greatest bear and speculator on Wall Street,
- The head of the world's greatest monopoly,
- A member of President Harding's cabinet.

It was said to be a celebration of their success and an opportunity to plan their future exploits and dominance. These were the captains of their respective industries and some of the most successful businesspeople of the era.

But how did things turn out for these distinguished gentlemen?

Within 25 years, all these great men had met a horrific end to their careers or their lives:

- The president of America's largest steel company, Charles Schwab, died a bankrupt man.
- The president of America's largest utility company, Samuel Insull, died penniless.
- The president of America's largest gas company, Howard Hobson, suffered a mental breakdown, ending up in an insane asylum.
- The president of the New York Stock Exchange, Richard Whitney, had just been released from prison.

- The president of the Bank of International Settlements, Leon Fraser, had taken his own life.
- The nation's greatest wheat speculator, Arthur Cutten, died penniless.
- The head of the world's greatest monopoly, Ivar Krueger the "*match king*," also had taken his life.
- A member of President Harding's cabinet, Albert Fall, had just been given a pardon from prison so that he could die at home.

And as for the Wall Street Bear, Jesse Lauriston Livermore, famous speculator in the stock and commodities markets, his end is the most tragic of all. A week after Thanksgiving in 1940, Jesse walked into the Sherry-Netherland Hotel in New York, had two drinks at the bar while scribbling something in his notebook, then proceeded to the cloak room where he sat on a stool and shot himself in the head. He was 62 and left behind $5 million, down from the $100 million fortune he had amassed just ten years earlier. [xlv]

And the note he had scribbled?

"*My dear Nina: Cannot help it. Things have been bad with me. I am tired of fighting. I can't carry on any longer. This is the only way out. I am unworthy of your love. I am a failure. I am truly sorry, but this is the only way out for me. Love Laurie.*"

There are three major lessons we can take from this parable:

1. Those who are on top now are not certain to finish in that position and are not guaranteed everlasting success or happiness.
2. Be careful whom you choose to idolize.
3. The life of a professional speculator is an unpleasant one, filled with highs and lows but ultimately unsatisfying and, in all probability, mentally ruinous. Look no further than the example of history's greatest speculator for proof of this.

Frequently Retail Associates who pursue gold (promotions, etc.) swap everything else significant in their lives for the chance to hold the gold ring. However, most of those eventually lose their material gains. Even though temporary success may come to numerous men and women who position the acquisition of wealth first, you are able to idly evaluate the quality of their lives by looking at their later years. After that it becomes much easier to see if they're a Jack Welch, Chairman & CEO, GE or Mike Abrashoff, Commander of the USS Benfold, or perhaps they are much more like Jeffrey Skilling, CEO of Enron or Bernard Ebbers, CEO of WorldCom.

There is an enormous amount of distinction between men and women who choose to pursue the gold and people who pursue the **Gold Standard 3.0** life that is supercharged with the Golden Rule:

Retail Associate That Only Pursue the Gold	Retail Associates Who "Choose" to Pursue the Gold Standard 3.0 Life
Ask, "What can you do for me?"	*Ask, "What can I do for you?"*
Make convenient decisions.	*Make character decisions.*
Sacrifice family for finances.	*Sacrifice finances for family.*
Develop a rationale for their actions.	*Develop relationships with their actions.*
Possess a "me-first" mindset.	*Possess "another first" mindset.*
Count their dollars.	*Count their friends.*
Base their values on their worth.	*Base their worth on their values.*

Marvin Ellison – Example of a Leader that Lives a Gold Standard 3.0 Life

Marvin Ellison is chairman, president and chief executive officer of Lowe's Companies Inc., a FORTUNE® 50 home improvement company with more than 2,200 stores and approximately 300,000 associates in the United States and Canada.

Marvin has more than 35 years of retail leadership and operational experience within Fortune 500 companies. Prior to joining Lowe's, Marvin served as chairman and CEO of J.C. Penney Co., where he delivered positive sales growth, reduced debt, and generated positive adjusted earnings per share.

He has extensive experience in the home improvement industry, having spent 12 years in senior-level operations roles with Home Depot Inc. Most notably he served as executive vice president of U.S. stores from 2008 to 2014, dramatically improving customer service and efficiency across the organization as he oversaw U.S. sales, operations, installation services, tool rental and pro strategic initiatives. Before Home Depot, Marvin spent 15 years at Target Corp. in various operational and leadership roles.

Marvin earned a bachelor's degree in business administration from The University of Memphis, where he currently serves on the board of trustees. He also holds an MBA from Emory University. Marvin serves on the board of directors for FedEx Corporation and the Retail Industry Leaders Association.

Marvin's professional and civic leadership has earned him many accolades; most notable are Barron's "Top CEOs" in 2021 and 2020, "2017 Father of the Year" by the National Father's Day Council, Fortune's 2016 "World's Greatest Leaders," and "Corporate Executive of the Year" in 2016 by Black Enterprise.

Marvin and his wife Sharyn are committed to being of service within their faith and communities, primarily through the support of organizations that promote higher education, self-empowerment, and excellence for minority youth.[xlvi]

About the Author

Kevin McNabb is a 38-year veteran (began September 1985) of the Direct Selling Profession, and he helps direct sales professionals (MLM, Network Marketing, Party Plan) recruit more distributors, generate more leads, and develop into top earners in their company by incorporating a personal development strategy into their lives and business, so that they are personally positioned to help themselves and others become financially independent.

Kevin is one of the most in-demand speakers on ethics, peak performance, and responsible marketing in North America. Kevin over the past 37 years has shared the stage with Anthony Robbins, Sir Richard Branson, Kim & Robert Kiyosaki, John C. Maxwell, Robert Rohm, Lisa Nichols, Paul Zane Pilzer, Bruce Wilkerson, Chris Widener, Andy Stanley, Dexter & Birdie Yager, Rich & Doug Devos, Jay & Steve Van Andel, Burke Hedges, Ron Ball, Brad & Kim DeHaven, Scott & MJ Michael, Ron & Toby Hale, Joe & Marybeth Markiewicz, Bill & Janice Kerr, Lennon Ledbetter, Frank & Joan Mazzeo, Mark Hughes, Randy & Valorie Haugen, Jim & Sherry Reed, Bill Childers, Tim Foley, George & Ruth Halsey, Jerry & Cherry Meadows, Ron & Georgia Lee Puryear, Jody & Kathy Victor, Rick & Sue Lynn Setzer and many more.

Kevin currently is an Assistant Store Manager in Mississauga, Ontario, Canada of a Rona, Inc. store (stylized as RONA) which is a Canadian retailer of home improvement and construction products and services, owned by U.S.-based private equity firm Sycamore Partners. Kevin began his retail career with Lowes Canada in early 2017 and resides in Etobicoke, Ontario with his daughter.

Kevin McNabb - Definition of Success

"Success to me is having the people in my life that know me the best (family friends, colleagues, customers, etc.), love and respect me the most. During that journey I will know my purpose in life; I will grow and reach my maximum potential, and continually sow seeds that benefit others. " - Kevin McNabb

End Notes

[i] Bad reputation: America's Top 20 most-hated companies - https://www.usatoday.com/story/money/business/2018/02/01/bad-reputation-americas-top-20-most-hated-companies/1058718001/

[ii] Here are 10 unethical retailers you should avoid buying from on Black Friday - https://www.rawstory.com/2016/11/here-are-10-unethical-retailers-you-should-avoid-buying-from-on-black-friday/

[iii] Five unethical companies - https://www.ethicalconsumer.org/retailers/five-unethical-companies

[iv] A Project of ProEthics Ltd., Ethics Scoreboard, http://www.ethicsscoreboard.com/rb_definitions.html

[v] Executive Leadership Foundation, Inc., Absolute Ethics: A Proven System of True Profitability (Tucker, GA., 1987) 22-23

[vi] Epistle to the Son of the Wolf, 30, quoted at http://reference.bahai.org/en/t/b/ESW/esw-2.html, 11 May 2013

[vii] Udana-Varga, 5, 1, quoted at www.thegoldenrule.net 11 May 2013
[viii] Mathew 7:12, quoted at www.thegoldenrule.net 11 May 2013
[ix] Analects 15:23, quoted at www.thegoldenrule.net 11 May 2013
[x] A version of the Golden Rule put into modern, non-religious terms that some people live by, quoted at www.thegoldenrule.net 11 May 2013
[xi] Mahabharata 5, 1, quoted in ibid.
[xii] The Traditions of Mohammed, quoted at www.thegoldenrule.net 11 May 2013
[xiii] Sutrakritanga 1.11.33, quoted at www.thegoldenrule.net 11 May 2013
[xiv] Talmud, Shabbat 31a
[xv] quoted at www.thegoldenrule.net 11 May 2013
[xvi] Shast-nashayast 13:29, quoted at www.thegoldenrule.net 11 May 2013

[xvii] Socially Irresponsible Companies with High Returns - https://www.dividend.com/how-to-invest/bad-for-your-health-good-for-your-portfolio/ - 20 October 2021

[xviii] 2019 Fortune 100 Best Companies to Work For, https://www.greatplacetowork.com/best-workplaces/100-best/2019 , 23 July 2019

[xix] 2021 Fortune 100 Best Companies to Work For, https://fortune.com/best-companies/2021/search/?bestcos_industry=Retail , 17 October 2021

[xx] Top 100 Retailers, https://nrf.com/resources/top-retailers/top-100-retailers , 17 October 2021

[xxi] Our Favorites from the World's Most Ethical

Companies: See Our Top 17 - https://greencitizen.com/ethical-companies/ - 20 October 2021

[xxii] The 30 Worst Things About Working in Retail, https://www.ranker.com/list/worst-things-about-working-in-retail/ejlinehan , 26 July 2019

[xxiii] United States Census Bureau, www.cencus.gov/popclock/ , 26 July 2019

[xxiv] Tony Robbins, Personal Power II, Day 6 – The Driving Force

[xxv] Tony Robbins, Personal Power II, Day 6 – The Driving Force

[xxvi] Ned Herrman, The Whole Brain Business Book (New York: McGraw-Hill), 1996

[xxvii] United States Census Bureau, quoted at www.census.gov/popclock/ 7 August 2019

[xxviii] Charles W. Christian, 10 Rules of Respect, quoted at www.businesswee.com/stories/2003-02-09/commentary-goodbye-to-an-ethicist , 09 August 2019

[xxix] BusinessWeek, Commentary: Goodbye to an Ethicist, quoted at www.businessweek.com/stories/2003-02-09/commentary-goodbye-to-an-ethicist 12 August 2019

[xxx] Fortune Magazine, CNN Money, 100 Best Companies to Wok For, quoted at www.money.cnn.com/magazines/fortune/best-companies/2013/snapshots/94.html?iid=bc_fl_list 12 August 2019

[xxxi] Human Capital 30: Companies that Put Employees Front and Center, https://fortune.com/2016/03/08/human-capital-30/ 12 August 2019

xxxii How A People-First Culture Is Changing How Leaders Manage Employees, https://www.forbes.com/sites/forbescoachescouncil/2016/07/01/how-a-people-first-culture-is-changing-how-leaders-manage-employees/#3ad5d01f2c87 12 August 2019

xxxiii J.C. Penney, Fifty Years with the Golden Rule (New York: harper and Brothers, 1950), 16
xxxiv Norman Beasley, Main Street Merchant (New York: Bantam, 1950), 63
xxxv J.C. Penney, Fifty Years with the Golden Rule (New York: harper and Brothers, 1950), 52
xxxvi J.C. Penney, Fifty Years with the Golden Rule (New York: harper and Brothers, 1950), 52
xxxvii Government Executive, Study: Ethical breaches becoming common in government, quoted www.govexec.com/pay-benefits/2008/01/stud-ethical-breaches-becoming-common-in-government/26192/ 22 August 2019
xxxviii U.S. Retailers Lead World in Data Breaches, https://www.retaildive.com/news/us-retailers-lead-world-in-data-breaches/528873/ , 22 August 2019

xxxix USDebtClock.org, quoted at www.USDEBTCLOCK.org, on August 30 2019
xl C.S. Lewis, Mere Christianity (San Francisco: Harper San Francisco, 2001), 122
xli Industry Week, People Who Cheat at Golf Cheat In Business, quoted at www.industryweek.com/corporate-culture/people-who-cheat-golf-cheat-business , 29 Aug 2019
xlii United States Census Bureau, quoted at www.census.gov/popclock/ 21 Oct 2019
xliii Jamaica national bobsled team, quoted at www.en.wikipedia.org/wiki/Jamaica_national_bobsled

_team 22 Oct 2019

[xliv] USA Today, WorldCom's whistle-blower tells her story, quoted at www.usatoday30.usatoday.com/money/companies/regulation/2008-02-14-cynthia-cooper-whistleblower_N.htm 23 Oct 2019

[xlv] Forbes.com, The Nine Financiers, a Parable About Power, quoted at www.forbes.com/sites/joshuabrown/2012/07/25/the-nine-financiers-a-parable-about-power/ 24 Oct 2019

[xlvi] Marvin R. Ellison – Chairman, President & Chief Executive Officer, Lowe's Companies Inc. - https://corporate.lowes.com/who-we-are/lowes-leadership/executive-leadership/marvin-r-ellison

www.ingramcontent.com/pod-product-compliance
Lightning Source LLC
Chambersburg PA
CBHW071402210526
45465CB00001B/213